Nov. 7, 2009

Welcome Home Hermana
Jackson! May the last
18 months be a period
in your life that you
treasure. Your missionary
service has blessed many
lives! Congratulations
and best wishes always.
Love —
Bishop Ostler

JOE J. CHRISTENSEN

BOOKCRAFT
Salt Lake City, Utah

To the thousands of missionaries
who have enriched the lives
of my wife and myself.

BOOKCRAFT is a registered trademark of Deseret Book Company.

Visit us at deseretbook.com

First printing in hardbound 1989
First printing in paperbound 1995

Library of Congress Catalog Card Number: 89-85673

ISBN 0-88494-705-X (hardbound)
ISBN-10 0-88494-981-8 (paperbound)
ISBN-13 978-0-88494-981-7 (paperbound)

Printed in the United States of America
R. R. Donnelly and Sons

10   9   8   7

Contents

When I accepted the invitation to write these suggestions for returned missionaries, I wondered about the narrow band of population who would be interested enough to read them. My next thought was that even though it was a narrow population band, I could think of no more important collection of people than returned missionaries. My wife and I now have sixteen grandchildren, and we hope and expect that there will be yet more. That is also a narrow band; but if no more than they read and follow these suggestions as they become returned missionaries, I will feel well rewarded for the effort.

It has been my privilege for more than forty years to observe missionaries. I have seen them before they were called—while I served as a bishop and as director of institutes of religion adjacent to several university campuses. My wife and I then had first-hand experience while I was presiding over the Mexico City Mission, during which time we came to know more than ever before that a powerful mantle accompanies the calling and that missionaries really are special.

Later, while I was serving as president of the Missionary Training Center, we saw young men and women by the tens of thousands—in fact, more than fifty-eight thousand—while they adjusted to their first weeks of missionary service. As parents, Barbara and I have been ever more personally involved as we observed all of our sons and all of those who became our daughters' husbands as they returned from their missions and went on with their education, marriages, careers, and families.

Lately, my opportunity to serve as president of Ricks College has given us the additional firsthand experience of seeing thousands of returned missionaries who are now pursuing their college educations. As a group, returned missionaries lend great strength to the student body. I have made it a point to watch them carefully as they adjust after they come home. I know that returning from a mission presents a challenge of adjustment—even for those who were the most successful while serving (and maybe especially for them).

Now, in light of all these years' experience, I have become convinced that there are some suggestions that can help you as you adjust to being home and proceeding with your life. You have tremendous promise in your future. If you follow correct principles, you can build on the great experiences you had in your missionary service and continue faithfully on the path of eternal life you have learned to love.

You who have returned home from missions, know that we respect you. We trust you. We have confidence that you will rise to the best that is in you. We love you for what you are and especially for what you will become now that you have returned. Like Alma, anyone who has waited at home and who loves missionaries will "rejoice exceedingly" to have them return, especially to see that they are "still his brethren [and sisters] in the Lord" (Alma 17:2–3).

Welcome home!

Acknowledgments

This book is not an official Church publication, and I assume complete personal responsibility for the views it expresses. Nevertheless I feel a deep need to express my appreciation to those whose writings I have cited, to those whose personal thoughts I have expressed, and to those who have given me encouragement in the project.

No book issues from a publisher without the assistance of many capable people. Among those at Bookcraft who have been particularly helpful in this project are Cory Maxwell, who first extended the invitation to tackle the writing task and along the way evidenced such patient and professional qualities; George Bickerstaff, whose suggestions and well-known editorial skills proved so beneficial; and other staff members who served in less visible but similarly helpful capacities.

I express appreciation also to Commissioner J. Elliot Cameron, Paul Hanks, and Preston Glade of the Church Educational System and to President Charles and Gay Grant for their careful reading and suggestions; and to Bonnie Brown Peterson, whose patient typing and retyping of manuscripts brought the final drafts to the point at which they could be submitted to the publisher.

Finally, I acknowledge the constant, loving support of my wife, Barbara, without whose encouragement and assistance very few of the truly meaningful things in my life would have been achieved.

The Importance of Being a Returned Missionary

Elder LeGrand Richards of the Quorum of the Twelve Apostles was one of the greatest missionaries of all time. When he was ninety-six years old, he no longer was able to drive his car. As a result, whenever he came to speak to the missionaries at the Missionary Training Center in Provo, Utah, we had the privilege of providing him with transportation.

On one of those trips, we asked, "Elder Richards, after all the years you have lived, all the places you have been, and all the things you have done, what do you consider to be the most significant experience of your life?"

He didn't hesitate for a moment in making his enthusiastic response, "Why, it was my first mission to Holland!"

He then proceeded to share with us some of the choice and challenging experiences he had when he left home and arrived in Holland without knowing a word of Dutch. He said that even the dogs understood the language, but he supposed that if the dogs could learn to understand Dutch, he probably could also. He did.

In his journal Elder Richards described some of the experiences he had at the end of his mission:

> In the evening meeting I spoke first to give my farewell. As I walked into the pulpit and viewed the faces of the brothers and sisters all sitting with awe to see what was to be said, a feeling came over me that I had never had before. To think how I had preached them the word of the Lord with all the power the Lord had given me. . . . I had learned to love them, and they in turn placed me far above what I really am. . . . I never in my life felt happier than under the influence of the Spirit present this evening. (As quoted in Tate, *LeGrand Richards,* p. 52.)

Just before leaving, Elder Richards went to the home of a woman who, with her family, had come into the Church as a result of his missionary efforts. His biographer describes the occasion:

> She was so short that she had to look way up to him. . . . When he went to leave, tears rolled down her cheeks and she said, "Elder Richards, it was hard to see my daughter leave for Zion a few months ago, but it is much harder to see you go."
>
> He went to bid another convert good-bye, a man who stood erect in the uniform of his country. This friend got down on his knees and took the elder's hand in his, hugged and kissed it, and bathed it with his tears of gratitude for the gospel the missionary had brought. Elder Richards said upon leaving him, "I wept all the way from Amsterdam to Rotterdam, thinking that I might never see those friends of mine

again. *It was much harder to leave them than it was my own family when I left on my mission.*" (Tate, *LeGrand Richards*, pp. 52–53; italics added.)

If your mission was a success, you probably had similar feelings. Leaving the mission field can be harder than entering. There may have been tears shed when you left home, but likely more tears were shed as you left the mission field knowing that you would probably never see many of the people again whom you came to love so much. You have gone through the most significant personal development possible for a young adult, an experience that has the potential to affect you for good from now on. You have paid the price of time and effort to help build the kingdom, to proclaim the gospel, to strengthen the stakes of Zion—or in the newest areas of missionary effort, to help lay the foundation for the establishment of the Church. You have responded to the call from a prophet of the Lord to lay on the altar a personal offering of a "tithing" of your life to this point, and now you are ready to see what you can do with the remaining time you have during your life's mission. As one mission president told his missionaries, "Your time in the mission field is the MTC to prepare you for the rest of your life."

You are special in the eyes of many people who have placed you on a pedestal. You have achieved that special status of becoming a "returned missionary" in a church that places great emphasis on missionary service and on the importance of sharing the message of the restored gospel of Jesus Christ. Many responsibilities rest upon you.

It is not surprising that the impact of a mission is so powerful. It has immersed you in a spiritual setting more deeply than you may ever again experience full time. You have gone through the unique experience a mission provides. That window in your life has now closed, and the time has come to look to the future, to move on, and to build on the foundation this life-changing experience has provided.

About missionary service we read:

> This is a marvelous plan. It is a process of sanctification. When a missionary is placed in a mission environment of order and discipline where all that is done is in harmony with the Spirit, the missionary experiences a great transformation. The heavens open. Powers are showered out. Mysteries are revealed. Habits are improved. Sanctification begins. Through this process the missionary becomes a vessel of light that can shine forth the gospel of Jesus Christ in a world in darkness. . . .
>
> Missions are for missionaries. It is a marvelous gift of time, a time given when you can experience glimpses of heavenly life here on earth. It is a time of cleansing and refreshing. It is a special time when the Holy Ghost can seal upon you the knowledge of the great plan for your exaltation. It is one of your best opportunities to become a celestial candidate. (William R. Bradford, in Conference Report, October 1981, p. 73.)

Some Church leaders have referred to a mission as the "University of the Lord." Any returned missionary who has followed the prescribed schedule has received more than seven thousand waking hours of specialized training in scripture, doctrine, teaching, leadership, and working in missionary service. It would take you more than fifty years of attending the regular three-hour Sunday block of Church services to receive an equivalent number of hours of training. Missionary experience and training are vitally important in a church which calls its leadership from among the regular members.

Alma Taylor, summarizing President Heber J. Grant's instructions as a mission president, wrote:

> One of the purposes of calling young men on missions was to open up communication between heaven and the missionary in order that when he returns home to Zion he may be worth something to the church and the Lord. He stated that President [Andrew] Kimball of the Saint Joseph Stake always kept as many of the young men as possible in the mission field for the reason that he needed strong men to help in the building up of a new country and realized that the best way to get them filled with the spirit is to have them on a mission for two or three years. Even if we do not baptize a soul we will be repaid for all the sacrifices we make in the abundance of other blessings we will receive. When the power of the evil one was threatening the church, when many of the prominent men were apostatizing, when the saints were receiving their bitterest persecution, the Prophet Joseph Smith sent the apostles on missions so that when they returned they would be filled with the power of God and be prepared for their mighty labors at home. If we can do our duty and go home with the proper spirit, we have obtained much and our labors will have been in no wise vain. (As cited in Gibbons, *Heber J. Grant,* pp. 128–29.)

As a result of this great growth experience, your life will never be the same. You have achieved a new status. You now have a title that can never be taken away from you. You will automatically be respected by many people merely because you are a "returned missionary," even though they know little or nothing of the quality of the service you rendered. Some will judge the Church for good or ill by your actions and your example. If you decide that you will accept the challenge of moving forward in the right directions, you will find deep joy and satisfaction in your future.

It is good to know that almost all returned missionaries manage to adjust and move on successfully with their lives. The few who do not generally suffer personal disaster. You should recognize that there are pitfalls ahead in almost every direction.

When one Elder was asked what made his adjustment and success so positive, he said: "I decided that it would be helpful if I served in the future after my mission just as I had been expected to serve in the mission field—with all my 'heart, might, mind and strength.' If I did that, I could be successful. I agree with my mission president, who said that in one sense I had not really been released at all, but rather just transferred to a new area of challenge and opportunity. The same principles that worked in the mission field apply at home, but it takes a lot of doing."

Commencement is a term used to describe the milestone of a student's graduation. Similarly, when you return from a mission, you arrive at the commencement of all that lies ahead of you. A new chapter begins in your life. All the pages are clean, and you now have the opportunity of taking all your mission experience and applying it to everything else you will be accomplishing.

Remember that "Alma did rejoice exceedingly to see his brethren; and what added more to his joy, they were still his brethren in the Lord; yea, and they had waxed strong in the knowledge of the truth; for they were men of a sound understanding and they had searched the scriptures diligently, that they might know the word of God. But this is not all; they had given themselves to much prayer, and fasting; therefore they had the spirit of prophecy, and the spirit of revelation, and when they taught, they taught with power and authority of God." (Alma 17:2–3.)

Now that you are home, we "rejoice exceedingly" and invite you to read, ponder, and then pay the price of effort needed to apply the practical suggestions in this book. As you do, your future will be more successful than you have ever experienced in your life up to this point.

2

Settling In at Home

The positive impact of having a missionary come home is il-lustrated by this mother's report: "Our home has really been a lot more spiritual since Dan returned from his mission. He has brought a whole new dimension of the Spirit, and he has done it in a way that everyone has appreciated. We thought that we were being blessed to have him in the mission field, and that was true, but it even seems better to have his personal influence right here at home. All the other children seem very responsive."

That reaction is experienced frequently, but unfortu-nately not frequently enough. Occasionally some tensions arise because conditions at home do not fit the mission-ary's expectations.

Years ago, Thomas Wolfe wrote a book entitled *You Can't Go Home Again.* One implied message of the book is that once you have left home for a significant length of time, you will have changed enough that you will never find home to be exactly as you left it—in great measure because you will have changed regardless of whether the circumstances at home have changed. You will look at everything through your new eyes of experience. Knowing this in advance, if you discover that things are not exactly as you remember them when you left, you will be better prepared to avoid the first disappointment some missionaries have. Young family members will have grown up. Teenage brothers or sisters may have become much more independent. Perhaps not everyone is as faithful and responsive as you remember them or as you think they should be. You need to be tolerant, patient, and understanding while still maintaining your own personal standards of conduct and Church activity.

One Sister missionary, upon arriving home from her mission, said, "It was hard for me to get adjusted to the fact that everyone at home was not living the gospel as well as I thought they ought to. I guess I had just forgotten or maybe hadn't paid that much attention before."

A mission tends to cause a person to be more sensitive to the gospel and to what is expected of members and even nonmembers. Occasionally, some of the hardest situations to cope with are within the missionary's own home. If this is the case for you, you have a real need to demonstrate sensitive diplomacy.

After the first few days of excitement at being home again were over, a returned missionary shared this experience with me: "I was disappointed that even though my folks were fairly active in the Church, we had never had a kneeling family prayer even though we regularly had the blessing on the food at mealtimes. I wondered how I could help get Dad and Mom to start it without embarrassing them or coming across as 'holier than thou.' My Dad had always been shy and retiring and was not of the sort to push in these areas. My grandparents didn't have regular family prayer when Dad was growing up. It just hadn't become part of their lives.

"Finally, I decided that a quiet visit with Mom and Dad when no one else in the family was around might be the best approach. I raised the subject by saying something like, 'Mom and Dad, it has been so good to get home again. I have always appreciated you both so much. Your support while I was on my mission was great, and I know that I can never fully repay you for such a choice opportunity. Since I came home, I have been wondering about one thing, though, and that is family prayer. While on my mission, I found that kneeling in prayer night and morning with my companions was a great strength to me. How would you feel about our having a kneeling family prayer—maybe just before breakfast and dinner? And, if you would like, I would be happy to offer it whenever you want to call on me.' "

In this case, his parents readily agreed. It was almost as though they felt relieved that he had raised the question. That little conversation started a whole new family spiritual tradition and has blessed their lives for years since. And their example helped even his married brothers and sisters in their own families as they in turn started the same practice.

Later, this young man was able to sensitively suggest that reading the scriptures together as a family—especially the Book of Mormon—would be a choice addition to their family habits. The parents responded in the same positive way. As a result, their family achieved a whole new level of spirituality.

Some missionaries return and are not as diplomatic as they should be around their family or ward; in the end they often offend the very people they would like most to assist.

One father said: "I don't know why it is, but Jim came home from his mission and has spent most of his time trying to straighten us out. He felt we were not reading the Book of Mormon together as a family as much as we should, and in general we are not living up to his standards. I hope the other kids don't resent the orders they are receiving."

In this case the parents did not appreciate the manner in which their son had approached them in his efforts to change things. Returned missionaries need to be careful and diplomatic or they might do more harm than good. If your parents resist even sensitive suggestions for family prayer, scripture reading, or Church attendance, one of the best approaches you can take is to quietly set the proper personal example and avoid offending these important people in your life. Sooner or later, others in the family will likely adopt your practices, recognizing the improvement that will come into their lives. In some situations where a family is less active or may even be nonmembers, the less said the better. Actions do speak louder—and more convincingly—than words.

A younger brother reported: "When I saw my older brother Jim getting up each morning—day after day—and reading a few minutes in the Book of Mormon, I decided that I would like to join him. It was hard for me at first because I really enjoyed sleeping in longer, but our discussions and reading really helped me to gain a testimony of the gospel. It was at that time that I came to know that I wanted to serve a mission and let others know about the gospel."

No conversions that occurred during this older brother's mission would be more important than helping his own brother gain a testimony—and all this happened as one of the bonuses that came to him after returning home from his mission.

One of your tasks will be to be very tolerant and understanding of those around you. Certainly your family deserves to be treated as sensitively as you would treat your most promising investigators.

When it comes to family chores, be sure to do your share—and then some—with a very positive attitude. The example you set in this area will be not only helpful to your parents but also of great value to your younger brothers and sisters who look to you for an example. Even though you may not have been giving that kind of cheerful help around the house before your mission, take a chance on it now that you are home. Your mother and father will likely be able to adjust to the surprise, and you will feel good about yourself for carrying your share of the load.

One mother paid this tribute to her son: "It used to be that I would get so tired of asking the kids to do their chores that I would often just do them myself, because I was finding it easier in the long run. Since David came home, he is such a help the way he dives into everything around the house, and I'm finding it rubbing off on the others. That's another value of a mission!"

As you allow the Spirit to guide you in your new challenges and as you exercise sensitivity and patience with those around you, you will find great peace and success in your efforts at home. In your own quiet and effective way, you really can have a positive influence on many around you as you return and settle into your new role as a returned missionary.

3

Your Welcome-Home Address

One bishop, while assigning a returned missionary to give his welcome-home address, mentioned: "One of the most important traditional opportunities that will come to you as a returned missionary will be to address the congregation in a sacrament meeting here in your home ward. No other speech you could have given in the ward up to this time has anywhere near the potential for having as great a positive impact on the listeners as this one. If the Spirit and content are there, an immense amount of good can be accomplished."

A missionary's welcome-home address can be a significant experience for all concerned. It is a very important opportunity, but some missionaries are much more successful than others in making their presentations.

We asked several individuals the question, "Well, how did you enjoy the returned missionary's welcome-home address at sacrament meeting today?" The following are some of the comments we heard:

One said: "The missionary really seems to have grown a lot, and I liked how he expressed appreciation for his parents. They sacrificed so much for him while he was in the field."

Another ward member said: "That was one of the finest welcome-home speeches I have ever heard. He had just the right balance between information, testimony, and spirituality. Even though he went to a mission where they don't baptize great numbers of converts, he really seemed to maintain his enthusiasm and brought home a tremendous spirit. I wish he had had more time."

In another situation, the response was, "Oh, it was all right, but I wish he hadn't said those negative things about the people where he served."

One of the high priests in the ward said, "I like it when a missionary tells us about his mission and how things are going in the Church in the area where he worked."

On a little more negative note, one ward member commented on another address, "It seemed to be too much of a travelogue for me and didn't fit as well as I would like in a sacrament meeting."

A member of a bishopric mentioned: "During his speech, I occasionally glanced at the faces of the deacons and teachers. I think that what he said really had a positive influence on the young men in the ward. There will likely be several who will have been influenced positively to consider a mission in their future. That is one of the great values of having a returned missionary speak in sacrament meeting."

A young woman home from college said: "My testimony was strengthened by her speech. She really brought a fine spirit into the meeting and, more than ever, caused me to consider going."

Returned missionaries, when you speak, remember that in the audience there will likely be parents, brothers, sisters, grandparents, aunts, uncles—the more and the less active. There will also be friends who have served missions (maybe a few from your own mission) and some who have not served. There will be neighbors of all ages, including deacons, teachers, priests, and girls of comparable ages who are at a very impressionable time in their lives.

The spirit and circumstances of a missionary's welcome-home address can touch hearts and change lives. Because of the emotions and attitudes that are generally present when a missionary reports his or her mission, there are those in attendance who are perhaps more likely to be influenced by the message and Spirit present than in most other Church meetings.

It is very natural for you to be a little nervous about your welcome-home address. One Elder admitted: "I don't know when I worried more about a speech. From the time I got on the plane to come home I thought about it. The bishop had written to let me know that two weeks after getting home would be the Sunday for me to report my mission."

Being a little nervous or anxious in this situation is not all bad. These feelings can help stimulate you to prepare better and to seek the Spirit more intently. If you are overly confident, your chance of doing all the good you could will be diminished. Here are some suggestions that can help you successfully meet this important challenge.

In the first place, remember the major objective of the meeting. You have the privilege of speaking in the sacred setting of a sacrament meeting that has among its primary purposes allowing the members to renew their covenants with the Lord by partaking of the sacrament, being taught the doctrines of the restored Church, and receiving renewed commitment to live its principles. You should not say or do anything that would distract from these outcomes.

All of these purposes can be achieved as well in a sacrament service that includes a missionary welcome-home address as in any other service. In fact, if the returned missionary does well, the real purposes of a sacrament meeting can be achieved perhaps even more easily than on most other occasions.

Since the time available to you is often short, express appreciation and love to your family and the ward members in the early part of your speech. Include a sincere, heartfelt expression of appreciation to your parents, family, Church leaders, and the ward members for what they have done to provide you with the opportunity and support to serve a mission. These expressions of love and appreciation will be among your most important messages. These significant people in your life will cherish them and never forget them. Saying how much you appreciate your parents and others will also be an important example for the younger members of the congregation to hear. Again, express appreciation early so that you will not forget to include it.

In the main body of your remarks, let the congregation know something of the country or area in which you served and how missionary work and the Church are progressing there. Avoid the temptation of taking too much time on this, thus turning this portion of your speech into a travelogue. This could rob you of time needed to share many of the spiritual experiences you had that strengthened your testimony of gospel principles.

The Savior, as the master teacher, was very effective in reaching his listening audience through experiences, parables, and examples. You can benefit from applying a similar approach. Include personal experiences that will let the congregation know of a few occasions on your mission when you knew that the Spirit was with you in the conversion of some of your investigators. Let the audience know how you felt as you shared some particular principle of the gospel or scripture that came to have special significance to you. You will note that the congregation's attention level will greatly increase when you include a personal interest example that also includes a gospel message.

One missionary added greatly to his speech by focusing on those mission experiences that taught him the value of faith in the gospel and the Lord Jesus Christ. While you served on your mission, you taught others the value of gospel principles. You saw how these principles blessed people's lives and changed them for good. Share with the congregation some of those experiences and you will bless many in the audience. You can teach powerful gospel principles in a very personal way that relates to the missionary experiences you had. As you share these experiences, you can feel great confidence because, of all people, you are the only real authority in reporting what you personally experienced and felt. If you focus on the experiences that strengthened your testimony of the restored gospel, in the process you will likely strengthen others.

This is a time to accentuate the positive. In the event that you served your mission in a developing or third-world country where the living standards, customs, and values were very different from your own, be sure that you keep your message on a positive note. If you were to comment disparagingly about the people you served or about the conditions in which you lived, you could do a great disservice to those in that mission field. Others in the audience whose attitudes and possible biases could be changed for the better by a more positive approach could also be affected negatively. Also, if you are not careful, some harm could be done to the younger members in the congregation who might next be called to serve among those same people. As a result, they may take with them some of the negative attitudes they received from you rather than the positive feelings they should have taken. You will not go wrong if you accentuate the positive.

One of the most important components of a successful welcome-home sacrament meeting message will be your testimony of the Savior, the restoration of the gospel of Jesus Christ through the Prophet Joseph Smith, and our Heavenly Father's plan of salvation and exaltation. From the depths of your heart and soul, share what you feel. Let there be no misunderstanding of where you stand when it comes to a testimony of the truth. Share with them what you have witnessed—that which the gospel can accomplish in the lives of converts to the Church. Express gratitude for the privilege of serving a mission as one of the Lord's emissaries, and urge others in the audience to take advantage of the same opportunity.

Occasionally, some missionaries wonder about how to deal with the second language they learned while serving in a foreign country.

One Elder said, "One of my concerns was what to do during my talk, if anything, with the Japanese I had spoken on my mission. I had heard other returning missionaries say a few remarks in their mission language, and I wondered what I should do. I didn't want to overdo it or underdo it."

For the interest of the congregation and further explanation of the culture of your mission, you may choose to say a few words in the language you learned. You might well consider bearing a *portion* of your testimony in it.

One bishop said, "I enjoy hearing a small part of a missionary's welcome-home address in the language he or she has learned. I think it is good for the younger people as well as those of us who are older. But I think that most of the missionary's testimony ought to be shared in the language of the congregation, and then everyone can more easily receive the confirmation of the Spirit that the message is true."

Follow these suggestions, pray diligently for inspiration, and then let the Spirit guide you. Your welcome-home address will strengthen those who listen. If handled properly, it can be a warm and special memory for you for the remainder of your life.

4

Adjusting Socially

At this point, let us consider some of the challenges and opportunities that lie ahead in the area of your successful social adjustment.

Elder Anderson had been home for two months when he said, "For me, I found getting back in the social swing of things was my most difficult readjustment." He would probably have agreed with Elder Paul H. Dunn, who wrote the following about social adjustments after a mission:

> Another problem is that he's been out of the natural environment of boy-girl relationships. Now he wants to relate to a young lady—or a sister wants to relate to a young man—but it's been taboo for two years; and all of a sudden to pick up a girl's hand in a car or a movie somewhere seems blasphemous, if not downright vulgar. So, he has a few

social adjustments to make. But we have found that if the ward or branch at home, the family, and the missionary work together, the adjustment is beautiful, sweet, and great. And for most missionaries, it really is a nice and casual adjustment with no problems except a few normal anxieties. (*New Era*, July 1971, p. 40.)

Of all the challenges for a returning missionary, none is listed more often than that of adjusting socially. For Mark, coming home was relatively simple from a social standpoint, in part because he had dated no one seriously before leaving for his mission. No one was at the top of his list. He had only written to a few high school friends once or twice. He said, "As far as I'm concerned, that is the *only* way to go!"

Even though being unattached to any certain girl may be simpler, the fact is that many missionaries do leave sweethearts at home who are very special to them; and although they were not formally engaged to be married, they may at least have had an agreement that he or she would be there when the mission ended. In describing his situation, one Elder said, "Well, some of them are there when the missionary returns and some are not. I don't think I will ever forget the day I received my 'Dear John.' It was really tough. Fortunately, I had a companion who helped me make that adjustment by working extra hard and getting her off my mind. I can see now that it was for the best in the long run, but it was hard to take at the time. Now that I'm home, I feel that I have to start all over."

One of the most difficult changes of pace faced by many young people called as missionaries is to leave dating, courtship, and social associations with members of the opposite sex. Biologically, a missionary at age nineteen and into the early twenties is at the time of life when the natural attraction toward members of the opposite sex is likely as high as it will ever be. It is most interesting that the Lord chooses this point in a young person's life to provide another of mortality's important tests. He calls young people on missions and, through his prophets, issues the guideline that during the time of a mission there will be no dating or courtship; indeed, the only allowable physical contact between a missionary and a member of the opposite sex will be a handshake.

There are those outside the Church who have difficulty in believing that young people at this time of their lives are expected to live up to this high standard of conduct. The amazing reality is that all the missionaries, with very few exceptions, rise to this challenge magnificently. They learn to control their natural biological urges and attractions; and by having done this, they prove to themselves and to others that they are in control of one of the most powerfully significant areas of their lives.

Missionaries who are successful in following this standard and who learn to control their natural romantic feelings will bring an established self-discipline into their marriages and homes. As Church members, we probably fail to recognize fully the immense value of such an achievement in helping marriages and homes to be more stable and, ultimately, to last through the eternities. The chances for moral unfaithfulness to destroy a marriage are greatly reduced when people who are in control marry. A mission provides excellent training in this area.

As mentioned above, if you are a young returning missionary, your girlfriend or boyfriend is either there waiting or isn't there at all. Regardless of the situation, challenges lie ahead for you in the area of dating, courtship, and, ultimately, finding one who will become an appropriate eternal companion for you.

For you Elders who feel that you had found "Miss Right" before your mission, and she is there at the airport waiting when you return, here is one piece of important advice: Don't rush into marriage too quickly. Recognize that changes will have occurred in both of you, and you need to become reacquainted. The intervening months of intense spiritual, physical, intellectual, and social developments have produced changes in both of you that neither fully understands. You need adequate time to see if you really feel the same way you did before your mission. If after an appropriate period of time for getting reacquainted you decide you are still in love, that is marvelous; but it could be that in this time of reacquaintance you will discover that you both would benefit from meeting some other possibilities.

One missionary's fiancée had even mailed out the invitations to their wedding reception before he was released from his mission. The trousseau had been bought and their first apartment rented. The wedding took place within one week of the missionary's return. Over the years, their marriage has not been what either of them would call ideal because of their lingering concerns that one or the other may have done better by "testing the waters" a little more before entering into an eternal commitment.

In addition to personal and social relationships, another reason for taking more time is to allow yourself to be further along in preparing to earn an appropriate living. Career preparation is a lot easier to accomplish without the obligations that come with a rushed marriage. (On the other hand, however, marriage and family should not be unnecessarily postponed until you have reached financial independence.)

There is no more important decision that you will make following your mission than to find and select the right marriage companion. Take sufficient time to make a good choice.

In the past there may have been a few mission leaders who have suggested that missionaries get home and quickly find the right companion and be married within six months, or within a year at the most. While marriage should not be postponed too long, it should also not be rushed. On this matter the General Authorities of the Church have clearly instructed:

> Priesthood leaders should counsel returning missionaries on the importance of continuing to live standards that will lead to celestial marriage. However, leaders should not recommend or imply that a missionary should marry within a specified time following his release. Although the returned missionary should keep himself worthy and moving toward marriage, the decision to marry is so important that he should make it only after the most prayerful and careful consideration. The post-mission period is one of social, emotional, and physical readjustment, with differing individual demands of employment and education. The returned missionary should not feel the additional pressure of time limits to make this very personal, sacred, and significant decision. (*Ensign,* April 1982, p. 79.)

There are some who seem to fear assuming the responsibilities involved in marriage and get into a social pattern that permits them to continue single for years beyond the ideal time. In so doing, they do not rise to their potential. President Ezra Taft Benson spoke very clearly on avoiding the extreme of postponing marriage too long:

> My dear single adult brethren, *we* are also concerned. We want you to know that the position of the Church has never changed regarding the importance of celestial marriage. It is a commandment of God. The Lord's declaration in Genesis is still true:

"And the Lord God said, It is not good that the man should be alone" (Genesis 2:18).

To obtain the fulness of glory and exaltation in the celestial kingdom, one must enter into this holiest of ordinances.

Without marriage, the purposes of the Lord would be frustrated. Choice spirits would be withheld from the experience of mortality. And postponing marriage unduly often means limiting your posterity, and the time will come, brethren, when you will feel and know that loss.

I can assure you that the greatest responsibility and the greatest joys in life are centered in the family, honorable marriage, and rearing a righteous posterity. And the older you become, the less likely you are to marry, and then you may lose these eternal blessings altogether.

President Spencer W. Kimball recounted an experience he once had:

"Recently I met a young returned missionary who is 35 years old. He had been home from his mission for 14 years and yet he was little concerned about his bachelorhood, and laughed about it.

"I shall feel sorry for this young man when the day comes that he faces the Great Judge at the throne and when the Lord asks this boy: 'Where is your wife?' All of his excuses which he gave to his fellows on earth will seem very light and senseless when he answers the Judge. 'I was very busy,' or 'I felt I should get my education first,' or 'I did not find the right girl'—such answers will be hollow and of little avail. He knew he was commanded to find a wife and marry her and make her happy. He knew it was his duty to become the father of children and provide a rich, full life for them as they grew up. He knew all this, yet postponed his responsibility." . . .

Honorable marriage is more important than wealth, position, and status. As a husband and wife, you can achieve your life's goals together. As you sacrifice for each other and your children, the Lord will bless you, and your commitment to the Lord and your service in His kingdom will be enhanced.

President Benson also reminded us:

Remember the counsel of Elder Bruce R. Mc-Conkie that "the most important single thing that any Latter-day Saint ever does in this world is to marry the *right* person in the *right* place by the *right* authority." (In Conference Report, April 1988, pp. 58–59.)

Striking the appropriate balance of not marrying too soon, or too late, will require the influence of the Spirit as you weigh decisions. Remember that time is on your side and that you can know when the right time comes.

Your chances for a successful marriage will be enhanced if you select a marriage partner who has been out of high school long enough to have lived through some of the maturing and growth experiences that only time can provide. Studies show that the younger the person, the more difficult their adjustment to the mature responsibilities that accompany marriage.

In a conversation with his mother, one returned missionary son produced a long list he had written and said: "When I marry, I want my wife to have these qualities: 'She must be beautiful, intelligent, not overweight, well-educated, like similar activities that I like,' and so on."

When he had finished reciting his long list, his mother said: "Son, remember that it is more important for you to focus on developing the qualities in your own life that you want to find in a mate and become the kind of person you are looking for. If you do, your chances of finding the right person will be much better. Think less of what the other person needs to be and a lot more about what you need to become. Then, watch for the person who brings out the best in you—the person who makes you feel that you want to be a better person than you are now. Ideally, marriage is the most important 'MIA' [Mutual Improvement Association] there is."

Young men may want to look for someone who knows basic homemaking skills, or at least is inclined to learn them. She doesn't need to be perfect; but in addition to whatever education she has, it surely helps if she is able to cook and sew and has the desire and commitment to maintain an orderly home. One farmer's marriage struggled even after several children had been born because the wife never was willing to spend sufficient effort to see that good meals were prepared on time and the laundry was done. The disarray in the house was always an embarrassment for him and the children.

By the same token, returned Sister missionaries would do well to look for a companion possessing basic home maintenance and repair skills, or at least one who is willing to learn them. If the husband has prepared himself to handle simple emergencies, he can ward off much discomfort and many unnecessary repair bills. Furthermore, a potential husband should be willing to help with cooking, washing dishes, and cleaning house—all traits he practiced regularly for at least the two years of his mission.

Ideally, the person you marry will share similar feelings to yours about having children and rearing a family. During courtship, a couple seriously considering marriage should discuss these attitudes and understand one another. In the final analysis, regardless of how rewarding a person's profession becomes, the deepest satisfactions and accomplishments are associated with family—spouse, children, and grandchildren.

A father remarked, "I used to think that when I became a father I would have a lot of influence with my children. Oh, sure I know that I have some influence, and I hope that it is good; but my job requires that I be gone from home during the working hours and occasionally I have to travel. It didn't take me long to recognize that it is my wife who has the greatest influence on our children. She is the one who spends the most time with them. I'm grateful to have every confidence in her and in how she will answer our children when they ask a lot of those tough questions that deal with the meaning of life, who our Heavenly Father is, why are we here on earth, and so on. Be sure to look for someone who has a deep testimony and understanding of the gospel, because in the long run your children will likely be influenced more by her than by you."

In addition to the social responsibility to find a choice eternal companion, you will likely need to locate new friends with whom to associate now that you are home. Often a missionary discovers that his or her friends have married or moved out of the area to go to school or work. Finding the right kind of associates is very important. Be sure to choose those who bring out the best in you.

One Elder reported: "When I came home, I found that most of my friends I knew before were either on their missions, away to school or work, or were married. I had to make some new friends. I found that when I was with friends who made it easy for me to live up to my standards, things went a lot better than when I always had to be on guard. Most of my friends are in the Church, but I have found some great nonmember friends who are of high standards and who keep my missionary feelings alive and well."

Another said: "When I got back into college, I found that becoming involved in our stake's young adult program and enrolling each semester in an institute of religion class were great places to meet new friends—male and female. They shared my values."

One returned missionary mentioned: "One of the choice contacts and experiences I have is to make the effort to attend our missionary reunions that are held at general conference time. I enjoy renewing contacts and friendships with some of the finest friends I know. They are the ones who really understand more of what I have experienced during those great years in the mission field. We have a lot in common. In fact, now that I think of it, if I really were in need of some help with some personal problem, the ones I would most likely be inclined to call are among those great friends I met in the mission field."

Now that you are home, you can put the social area of your life all together in a very constructive way by following these guidelines along with others you may feel are important for you.

5

Successful Dating

Everyone wants to be happy and successful. No one wants to fail, especially in life's most important decision of marriage. Hopefully, you are seriously committed to being successful in your dating and courtship so that you will arrive at the temple worthy to enter into a happy, eternal marriage. Throughout the years, many suggestions have come from Church leaders who have witnessed the personal successes of the majority of returned missionaries, as well as the occasional disasters that occur.

If you follow sound counsel, you will be protected and avoid what Elder Boyd K. Packer described in a general conference address as the "spiritual crocodiles" that present serious dangers if you are not careful:

> Those ahead of you in life have probed about the water holes a bit and raise a voice of warning

about crocodiles. Not just the big, gray lizards that can bite you to pieces, but *spiritual crocodiles*, infinitely more dangerous, and more deceptive and less visible, even, than those well-camouflaged reptiles of Africa.

These spiritual crocodiles can kill or mutilate your souls. They can destroy your peace of mind and the peace of mind of those who love you. Those are the ones to be warned against, and there is hardly a watering place in all of mortality now that is not infested with them.

On another trip to Africa, I discussed this experience with a game ranger in another park. He assured me that you can *indeed* hide a crocodile in an elephant track—one big enough to bite a man in two.

He then showed me a place where a tragedy had occurred. A young man from England was working in the hotel for the season. In spite of constant and repeated warnings, he went through the compound fence to check something across a shallow splash of water that didn't cover his tennis shoes.

"He wasn't two steps in," the ranger said, "before a crocodile had him, and we could do nothing to save him."

It seems almost to be against our natures, particularly when we are young, to accept much guidance from others. But, young people, there are times when, regardless of how much we think we know or how much we think we want to do something, that our very existence depends on paying attention to the guides. (*"That All May Be Edified,"* p. 210.)

Here are a few suggestions from some of the "guides" who can help you avoid the "crocodiles" that could destroy you.

Don't make a game of sharing physical expressions of affection. President Kimball taught the following:

> Among the most common sexual sins our young people commit are necking and petting. Not only do these improper relations often lead to fornication, pregnancy, and abortions—all ugly sins—but in and of themselves they are pernicious evils. . . .
>
> . . . If our young people would avoid the pitfalls . . . , kissing would be saved at least until these later hallowed courtship days when they could be free from sex and have holy meaning. . . . (*The Miracle of Forgiveness*, pp. 65, 231.)

> A kiss is an evidence of affection. A kiss is an evidence of love, not an evidence of lust—but it can be. Don't ever let a kiss in your courtship spell lust. Necking and petting are lustful; they are NOT love. . . . I don't mind your kissing each other after you have had several dates, . . . not the kiss of passion, but the kiss of affection and there won't be any trouble. Now remember these things.
>
> Even if timely courtship justifies the kiss, it should be a clean, decent, sexless one. ("Chastity.")

Avoid being alone as a couple in situations that may lead to your downfall. These include parked cars, especially in poorly lighted places. Many couples have begun an innocent discussion in a parked car and have unintentionally become physically involved to the point of moral disaster.

The automobile is still a challenge, but, in addition, in these times it has also become fashionable among some to be alone in each other's homes or apartments. You would be wise to determine right now that you will never go into a home or apartment with your date alone, and certainly never into the bedroom. If you will discuss, understand, and accept this standard early in your courtship, you can bypass many hazardous problems. Always avoid even the appearance of evil, and you will be protected.

Inappropriate videos and television programs add to the problem. What could be more dangerous than for a couple to enter a home or apartment alone and stretch out in front of the television set to watch an inappropriate video filled with lurid sexual scenes? One stake president of long experience said:

> I have had many members (young and old) tell me that they just "overlooked the filth in a movie and did not let it affect them adversely." To that I say, *Baloney!* You cannot go to a movie or to any entertainment which portrays sexual or violent materials, as do most movies today, and not be affected and spiritually hurt. It affects you whether you like it or not! In fact, if you find that this kind of material does not offend you, then this is a sure sign that you have already been spiritually damaged in your life and do not even know it. (Tingey, "Celestial Dating.")

If you are normal, you cannot overlook the impact of sexually stimulating scenes entering your mind and system. Avoid that sort of stimulation as you would a plague and you will be protected. Ignore caution in this area and you will be trapped like so many others into situations that get beyond your control—and disaster will occur. Few areas are infested with more "spiritual crocodiles."

A father was counseling a recently returned missionary son, who was dating the beautiful young woman he had dated prior to his mission. They were getting to the point that they were seeing each other almost every day and were talking of marriage.

"Spencer, this is a time in your courtship when you need to be particularly careful and be sure to not stay out too late. Never be alone in each other's home or apartment."

"Dad, there's *no* worry."

To which the father responded, "Spence, if I thought that I had a son who could be with an attractive young woman for long periods of time, alone in some romantic setting, and have no cause to worry about the possibility of their becoming inappropriately involved, then I would *really* be worried! There would obviously be something wrong with how your system is wired."

The natural biological attraction that exists between a healthy young man and woman makes this a time to be extremely cautious. Even as a returned missionary, you are not immune from the powerful influences of the hormones that course through your system; and, if not controlled, they can lead to the cause of your downfall. The adversary's tool of immorality may be old and worn, but it is still very effective in achieving his diabolical objectives. All you have to do to become a victim is to let down your guard and become careless.

The counsel against the negative effects of immorality comes not only from the prophets and Church leaders but also from wise people outside the Church. Will and Ariel Durant, the famous historians, were right when they wrote:

> A youth boiling with hormones will wonder why he should not give full freedom to his sexual desires. If he is unchecked by custom, morals or laws, he may ruin his life before he matures sufficiently to understand that sex is a river of fire that must be banked and cooled by a hundred restraints if it is

not to consume in chaos both the individual and the group. (*The Lessons of History,* pp. 35–36.)

Norman Vincent Peale wrote:

Life is so arranged that morality and happiness go hand in hand. . . . Immorality doesn't work, it doesn't pay off. It doesn't lighten the burden of living. It increases it. . . . Sex is too powerful, too profound, too elemental a force to be treated lightly or casually. It's like nitroglycerin—useful so long as it is protected and safeguarded, deadly if it is mishandled or abused. . . . I believe, myself, that the sexual restraints devised by society are an unconscious manifestation of the wisdom of the human race—they deepen erotic power by controlling and focusing it, and the resulting energy drives mankind upward along the path of civilization. (*Sin, Sex, and Self-Control,* pp. 73, 74, 92, 95.)

Do not dress immodestly—neither you nor your date. You have heard this counsel for years, but it has never been more important than it is right now in this period of your life. These days, designers of dress styles and fads seem to go all out for that which is immorally suggestive. President Kimball, who has given us so much good advice in these areas of danger, added:

I see some of our LDS mothers, wives, and daughters wearing dresses extreme and suggestive in style. Even some fathers encourage it. I wonder if our sisters realize the temptation they are flaunting before men when they leave their bodies partly uncovered or dress in tight-fitting, body-revealing, form-fitting sweaters. . . .

We cannot overemphasize immodesty as one of the pitfalls to be avoided if we would shun temptation and keep ourselves clean. (*The Miracle of Forgiveness*, pp. 226–27.)

In addition, you would be very wise to avoid letting yourselves get into physical positions that can lead to difficulty. For example, do not lie down by each other.

Lying down to watch television, lying down in the park, on the beach, or wherever, places you in a position that is not needed and spiritually unhealthy. When you watch TV, SIT UP! When you go on a picnic, SIT UP! When you have a good night kiss, at the proper time in a relationship, don't recline to do it. (Adapted from "Standards for Dating.")

Dating with other couples or in a group is not only safer but also much more instructive in helping you learn what you need to know about your partner, such as how your date relates with others. Some of your most important observations about your partner will come to you when you are in the presence of others. Some important personality traits and characteristics are more difficult to learn about if you are always alone. One observer said, "Never marry anyone until you have served on a major committee together."

There is a tendency for couples to almost withdraw from society when they feel they are becoming serious. Many begin to date almost exclusively alone. When they go to a dance, they dance only with each other all evening. To some this may seem more fashionable and, for a variety of reasons, more natural. These can be dangerous mistakes.

Absolutely avoid late hours. Your chances for coming through this time of dating and courtship in the best possible way are greatly enhanced if you will decide to not stay out late. How about not staying out beyond 12:30 A.M.? That probably seems too early to many who consider themselves of age to stay out as long as they choose. In reality, most proper functions will end by 12:00 midnight, and that leaves you with thirty minutes to get home. Do it, and you will be blessed.

At this point in your life, you probably do not feel that you need a long discourse on how your resistance is lower when you are both tired. Most moral problems—though not all—occur after young people have become familiar with each other during the course of the evening and late at night when it is harder to keep up their guard. So, to you young men, take her home, leave her there, and get to your own home by 12:30 A.M. Don't spend time in the parked car, on the porch, or in her living room. You young sisters can apply the same principles with your dating partners. Do what Joseph in the Old Testament did when faced with a tempting situation—he "got him out" (see Genesis 39). If King David had done the same, history and his own life both here and hereafter would have been greatly changed for the better. You will likely never know what advantages will come to you by simply following this practice of getting home early.

Have a discussion with your dating partners about the standards and safeguards you will mutually observe in your dating. Do it when your minds are clear and unhampered by emotions. Choose the high standards you should follow. If your partner does not agree with you, that is a good sign that you are with the wrong person and you ought to look elsewhere.

One of the most important realizations for the returned missionary is that anyone can fall into moral transgression. No one is exempt. This can be particularly true for those who have been away from the dating scene for many months. You need to exercise extreme caution in order to avoid the pitfalls. President Kimball's advice continues to be timely: "In your dating and courting, fully maintain the standards of the Church. Be morally clean. 'Let virtue garnish [your] thoughts unceasingly.' " (See D&C 121:45.)

You may have other cautions you will want to add to this list; but meanwhile, put the above into practice in your dating and courtship. If you will, you will be on your way to an enjoyable and exhilarating time of your life; furthermore, you will make a sounder foundation for this most important decision about whom you will marry. And you will more surely help your future marriage to last throughout the eternities.

6

Dress and Grooming

How you appear makes a real difference in how you feel about yourself. Your dress and grooming make a statement to others. You would be wise, therefore, to recognize that you should dress and groom yourself in a way that reflects your lifelong commitment to share the gospel. Peer pressure and modern fads will urge you to join a multitude of "grubby" dressers. Some missionaries, when they are freshly returned home, have questions about their dress and grooming. A few, because of insecurities, feel a need to give heed to the pressures and fads.

Those who may have wondered about the reasons behind the dress and grooming standards expected of missionaries should know that sensitive professional people outside the Church recognize the basic values found in the conservative missionary-type dress and grooming. Adopting these standards of appearance can be helpful far beyond the time that you serve in the mission field.

John T. Molloy is considered to be a "wardrobe engineer" who consults with many of the notable political and business leaders in America. He is the author of a best-selling book, *Dress for Success*. It is a book that could be profitably read by all returned missionaries who are hoping to be successful in a highly competitive business world.

Following are some opinions written by this same non-member professional wardrobe consultant that illustrate how sound the missionary dress standards for Elders are, including white shirts, ties, conservative suits, and clean-cut grooming:

> Clothes do make the man—in more ways than most suspect. Our firm has researched thousands of wardrobe combinations in psychological tests and found correlations between clothes styles/color and first impressions. The results are so consistent that we're able to develop formulas to provide various images to match various needs. Some examples:
> ... White shirts, ... are a sign of authority and credibility. ...
> Suit colors fit similar patterns. *Dark blue and gray suits read authority, credibility—a man who knows where he is going.* ...
> ... But the output measurements (of secretaries) found that *secretaries with bosses who wore dark blue/gray suits outperformed the others markedly.*
> ... *Facial hair (beard, moustache, long sideburns) detracts from credibility.* (Molloy, "Clothes Power"; italics added.)

I am impressed that effective professionals outside the Church so clearly recognize the value of the same dress and grooming standards that the missionaries follow as a result of inspired missionary rules. The fact is that around the world, missionaries are respected and admired for their appearance. It is an acceptance level that you would be wise to maintain now that you are home. That does not necessarily mean that you need to wear a suit in everyday class and work settings, but having a concern for your appearance clearly can lead to increased success.

Teenagers dress according to current fads in part to impress each other. You have come to a time in your life when it is important to dress in such a way that you can make a positive impression on those who may be in a position to place great confidence in you in work situations and in other positions of trust and responsibility. The impressions you make on them could greatly affect how they respond to you.

William Thourlby too is a clothing consultant. He has advised two United States presidents as well as key executives of many companies. You may not agree with all his conclusions, but you may find value in this selection of his thoughts:

When you step into a room, even though no one in that room knows you or has seen you before, they will make ten decisions about you based solely on your appearance. They may make many more, but you can be assured that they will make these:
1. Your economic level
2. Your educational level
3. Your trustworthiness
4. Your social position
5. Your level of sophistication
6. Your economic heritage
7. Your social heritage
8. Your educational heritage
9. Your success
10. Your moral character

To be successful in almost any endeavor, you must be sure that these decisions about you are favorable, because in that first impression you make —you are what you wear. If you realize that your inner image is reflected in what covers up 90 percent of you—your wardrobe—you'll be able to take advantage of the situation. . . .

The truth is we live in a "street culture." When people meet or see you for the first time, they make decisions about you based on that first impression. They rarely, if ever, change those first decisions. (From *You Are What You Wear*, pp. 1–3. Used with permission.)

As a thoughtful returned missionary, you will want to project the right message to friends, strangers, and particularly to the young prospective missionaries—the boys who look up to you and watch your example. You will want everyone to know that you are serious about the spiritual importance of what you have been doing. It is important for them to receive positive reinforcement from you about the values of the restored gospel and the privilege it is to share them with others. You will want to be credible and respected. You would not want someone else to think less of the importance of following gospel principles merely because you choose to slip back into premission fads in dress and grooming.

William Thourlby went on to write about the importance of clothing:

As the Queen of England [Victoria] wrote to her son, the Prince of Wales, "Dress gives one the outward sign from which people in general can and often do judge upon the inward state of mind and feeling of a person; for this they *can* see; while the other they cannot see. On that account, clothes are of particular importance, particularly to a person of high rank."

If clothes and what they say about one are that important to the Queen of England, who obviously cannot rise much higher, how important can they be to those of us who are reaching for opportunity. (From *You Are What You Wear*, pp. 15–16. Used with permission.)

President Kimball had some strong feelings about the dress and grooming of returned missionaries. Speaking to several thousand of them assembled at Brigham Young University, he included these significant remarks:

Sometimes we find a returned missionary who lets his hair grow long immediately. He is very anxious to become part of the world again. He has been free of the world for a couple of years, now he would like to taste that "sweet" world, if you can call it that. We find that some young men who return home from their missions put on their overalls the very first day they get home, and that old sweater that was ready to throw away before they left. They like to put on all those things. It always pleases me when I go to a community and I see the returned missionaries still well dressed, well groomed, and have their testimony and are eager to give the message that they had been teaching all those years.

I want you to know it is hard for me to be disappointed, and I rejoice in the blessings of the Lord daily. But a few things disappoint me occasionally and one of them is the returned missionary who, after two years of taking great pride in how he looks and what he represents, returns to this campus or some other place to see how quickly he can let his hair grow, how fully he can develop a moustache and long sideburns and push to the very margins of appropriate grooming, how clumpy his shoes [can] get, how tattered his clothes, . . . how close to being grubby he can get without being refused admittance to the school. That, my young returned missionary brethren, is one of the great disappointments in my life.

I meet with prime ministers and presidents, with sovereigns and rulers, political and public figures all over the world and one of the things they inevitably say about us (and always with warmth and appreciation) is, "We have seen your missionaries. We've seen them all over the globe, in every state and every district of the union and in most countries of the world. Without exception, they look like young men ought to look. They are clean cut, neatly dressed, well groomed and most dignified." My, that makes me proud! I'm trying to do my own little part in missionary work and that kind of comment makes me *so very* proud of our 26,000 missionaries. Then sometimes these great leaders say, "Your missionaries look like just the kind of young man I would want to take in my business, or in my government, or in my embassy, or in my law firm." Sometimes they even say, "They look just like the young man I would like to have for a son-in-law." That makes me proudest of all.

Please, you returned missionaries and all young men who can understand my concern in this matter, please do not abandon in appearance or principle or habit the great experiences of the mission field when you were like Alma and the sons of Mosiah, as the very angels of God to the people you met and taught and baptized. We do not expect you to wear a tie, white shirt, and a dark blue suit every day now that you are back in school. But surely it is not too much to ask that your good grooming be maintained, that your personal habits reflect cleanliness and dignity and pride in the principles of the gospel you taught. We ask you for the good of the kingdom and all those who have done and yet do take pride in you. (*The Teachings of Spencer W. Kimball,* pp. 592–93.)

In summary, always be sure that you are neat and clean in your dress. Your clothing does not need to be expensive or new, but you can see to it that it does not have the careless, grubby look that makes a negative statement about common standards of conservative dress.

Don't yield to the temptation to revert to premission, juvenile styles you left behind when you entered the mission field, even though there may be some among your acquaintances who encourage you to abandon your clean-cut dress and grooming standards. You will want and need the respect of substantial people, and these will regard you more highly if you maintain a well-groomed appearance. Among them could be one you will come to care about most, one who is looking specifically for an eternal companion with high standards—definitely a returned missionary. If your dress and grooming are faddish and worldly, you will more than likely attract social contacts who are also faddish and worldly.

Don't feel an obligation to follow any of the far-out clothing fads that may be current now that you are home. Rest assured that in a few months they will have changed. You need not be at the mercy of those who create the fads in Paris, California, New York, or wherever. You can be your own person when it comes to the clothes you wear. You can assure yourself that the impressions you make with your dress and grooming are advantageous to you and consistent with the significant assignment you have fulfilled as a minister of special truths in your mission field.

7

Choosing Your Life's Work

One of your most important challenges will be to decide how you are going to make a living—both during this time of adjustment and also in training for your life's work. What goods or services will you provide for which people will be willing to pay so that you can support yourself and, in time, a family? For some, these questions can become frustrating, to say the least.

One returned missionary said: "Before my mission, I put a lot of effort into preparing for it and not much thought into what I would do with my life after I got home in order to make a living for that future wife and family I hope to have some day. One of my biggest problems is that I don't know what to study at college."

The choice of your life's work should be considered among the most important decisions you will make. Robert D. Lock has shared this insight:

If someone were to speak to you about a subject that concerned a third of your life, a million dollars, your identity as a person, your way of life, and your physical and mental health, would you listen? The subject in this case is your career. You give the best years of your life to the work you do. Your jobs give you the means by which you make a living. You are identified by the occupations you practice. Your life-style is primarily dependent upon your occupation. A significant portion of your physical and emotional health is determined by how well you like your work. The activities at which you spend your time, the money you earn, who you are as a human being, the way you live, and your health compose the essential core of your existence. Because the study of careers covers so much of life itself, it is hard to imagine a subject more fundamental than this one.

Yet an overwhelming majority of people probably give very little thought to planning a career. Because they don't know how to go about it, many people avoid or ignore thinking about their career choices in the hope that they will somehow "luck out." Some may be lucky and find the right kind of work, but luck is usually a case of being prepared for opportunity. Far too many people drift into the world of work and then drift from job to job. They have only a series of jobs, not a career. . . .

The effort you put into career planning can lead to great rewards, both psychological and financial. There is a lot at stake here. You gain an identity from your occupation. You can fulfill yourself as a worker and contribute something to the world. There is a big investment in time; if you average 40 hours for 40 weeks over 40 years on the job, that's 64,000 working hours. If your yearly average income is $25,000 in that time, you'll be a millionaire in earnings. What you do at work determines much of what you do with the non-work parts of your life. Work is at the very heart of life. The French writer Albert Camus made the following observation about working: "Without work all life goes rotten. But when work is soulless, life stifles and dies." Need we say more about the importance of our subject? (From *Taking Charge of Your Career Direction*, pp. 2, 5. Copyright © 1988 by Robert D. Lock. Used by permission of Brooks/Cole Publishing Co.)

For many missionaries, finding an immediate income is a major difficulty. While in the mission field, most missionaries are spared the concern about these mundane matters and are generally free to focus their full-time attention on missionary work and sharing the gospel. While you were serving, your housing, food, transportation, clothing, and other essentials were generally taken care of from your missionary savings account, the support from your family, other generous people, or some combination of sources.

Now that you are released, it is different. You may be among those who do not have the financial resources you need right now to take care of expenses such as college tuition, housing, meals, transportation, clothing, and similar expenses. If this is the case, getting a job immediately may be among your most pressing priorities. Check all possibilities and take advantage of whatever honorable job may be available in the area in which you are living. Don't be too fussy. Any work that provides needed services to the community is not beneath you. In fact, some of the most important lessons of your life can be learned in what you may consider the most menial of tasks. But keep your eyes on your goals.

One returned missionary who got a job helping a farmer load and stack baled hay said: "On those hot, dusty

afternoons when the perspiration would run down my fore-
head into my eyes and when it seemed like there were
more bales of hay than energy, it was helpful to me to re-
mind myself regularly of the scripture, 'In the sweat of thy
face shalt thou eat bread, till thou return unto the ground'
(Genesis 3:19). Somehow, I felt better just knowing that the
Lord intended that we should work and exert effort while
we are here in this life."

Experience on the job is a valuable source of education. A returned missionary who is now very successful in
his profession said, "Every full- and part-time job I had following my mission gave me a lot better idea of what I
wanted to prepare myself to do with my life. I learned some
of my best lessons about work and the value of money that
I don't know I could have learned better in any other way."

Plan to get some training beyond your high school education that will best prepare you to earn a respectable living and which will enable you to contribute positively to
society. What will that be? It could be almost anything that
is honorable. You must sort out from a multitude of possibilities the area of preparation that will be best for you.

In addition to careers that require a college degree,
many others can be prepared for in technical schools and,
in some cases, through on-the-job training. Whatever you
choose, the job ought to be a means to a life of service. As
President Kimball counseled:

> You are not going to be satisfied, I am sure, with
> merely preparing to make a living, important as that
> is, but it must be secondary to the great and impor-
> tant thing of helping the Lord to bring to pass the
> immortality and eternal life of man, unselfish service.
> I would hope that you who are training to be teach-
> ers would not be learning to teach for the compensa-
> tion that would come each month, but that you

might inspire people throughout your lifetime, that you might build faith and build character in many. I would hope that you who are following other fields of endeavor, that your education and your employment would be a means to an end and not the end in and of itself. . . . Do great things for the glory of God and for the benefit of mankind. (*The Teachings of Spencer W. Kimball,* p. 257.)

A prime indicator of a good choice of occupation is to find a life's work that you would be pleased to do even if you were not paid a salary (and then receive one as an added bonus). Generally, such a choice will be in an area in which you have some natural talent and interest and will make your training and studies much more productive and enjoyable. Some people have interests in areas in which they are not particularly talented, and others have talents in areas wherein they are not especially interested.

One returned missionary said: "I studied and chose to go to work in accounting and was fortunate enough to find what I thought was a good job. After a few years I found that my work was not as satisfying as I had hoped. For me, leaving to go to the office each morning was sheer drudgery. The pressures of the job bothered me, knowing that I was responsible for many decisions and directions the company was taking in financial areas. I didn't feel good about a few of them, but I was obligated to carry out the assignments my bosses gave me. I also discovered that I often found the detailed work in accounting to be boring to me.

"Finally, I decided that life was too short to go on like that. My wife noticed that I was becoming a lot more irritable around home than I knew I should be. It was a scary thing to do, but I finally took the leap and changed my profession. It required some effort and sacrifice of salary to make the shift, but now I go to work every day looking forward to being there. Much of the negative pressure has evaporated, and my wife has noticed that I'm a lot more tolerable to live with."

This experience has nothing to do with accounting being a poor choice for everyone; there are accountants who find their work to be very challenging, rewarding, and fulfilling. To illustrate the point, one friend told me: "In my other job, I had to be working with the public all the time. The sales supervisor was always putting a lot of pressure on us, and I didn't enjoy making presentations in front of people. It began to eat on me, and I'd find that I wasn't sleeping as well as I should be. Now that I have changed and keep the books for my company, I am a lot more content."

Each person's talents and interests are different, and you need to discover which are yours and then take advantage of them. Fortunately, there are interest inventories and aptitude tests easily available in guidance centers—in colleges, personnel departments of many large companies, and also employment agencies. Without pressure and on your own schedule you can take the tests and then have a qualified counselor interpret the results for you. In this way you can find out a wide variety of suggested occupational choices that will fit your particular combination of talents, abilities, and interests. If you get your talents and interests together in your career choice you can save yourself a lot of time and frustration in your preparation and work experience. Remember, try to find some line of work you would be happy to do even if you didn't receive pay, and then you will be even more content when a salary comes with it.

The choice of a career is so important that you are well advised to make the decision a matter of fasting, prayer, and searching. Regular visits to the temple with this question in mind can provide a setting for inspiration to assist you. In the end, the Lord will probably allow a wide range of latitude in this area of your decision making and will leave much of the choice up to you. A wise decision will affect positively your life's direction and that of your family for years to come.

All of this searching for your life's work must be accompanied by a good portion of reality. Study where the opportunities for employment are. It does little good to prepare yourself for a career and find that there are no job openings in the area you would like to live in—or anyplace else, for that matter.

Once you have found some career choices that seem interesting to you, contact individuals you know who are successful in that line of work. Ask for an appointment to go to their office or wherever they work and visit with them about what they do, how they feel about it, its strengths and drawbacks, required training, and the best way to get hired. This will be one of the best investments of time you can make in terms of getting a more realistic feeling about the work or profession that seems attractive to you.

There are hundreds of very adequate colleges and universities that offer the degrees you may choose to seek. Some are obviously better than others. You should study their offerings carefully to determine which will meet your career needs. Where you can, visit with individuals who have attended the school and majored in the area you are considering. Ask specific questions about the quality, courses, faculty, costs, living environment, strengths, and weaknesses. Then make your decision.

In this day and age of rapid developments, don't feel that whatever you choose to do is a decision made in concrete. Studies show that the average person in America changes jobs more than once in a working career as some jobs are phased out and new opportunities are developed. If in your education and training you have developed some good general skills, you can be flexible.

Remember that your life will likely go on into the twenty-first century. In the past a person could do fairly well in making a living without formal training beyond high school. My father did well in his day with just eight years of schooling. The chances for that to occur in the upcoming years is much less likely. Become as well trained as your abilities and interests permit, and you will bless yourself and your future family.

8

Continue Learning and Keep a Balance

As a member and potential leader in the Church, you are expected to learn and prepare in a wide variety of areas. Consider again the significance of this scriptural counsel:

> Teach ye diligently and my grace shall attend you, *that you may be instructed more perfectly* in theory, in principle, in doctrine, in the law of the gospel, *in all things that pertain unto the kingdom of God,* that are expedient for you to understand;
>
> Of *things* both *in heaven* and *in the earth,* and *under the earth; things which have been, things which are, things which must shortly come to pass; things which are at home,* things which are *abroad;* the *wars* and *perplexities* of the nations, and the *judgments* which are on the land; and a *knowledge also of countries and of kingdoms*—

That ye may be prepared in all things when I send you again to magnify the calling whereunto I have called you, and the mission with which I have commissioned you. (D&C 88:78–80; italics added.)

It is hard to imagine such a broad description of areas of learning in so few words. Learning should become one of your prime objectives for as long as you live. Read and study widely. That is one of the purposes of the general education requirements that form the basis of most undergraduate degree programs in colleges today. In those programs, a student is required to fulfill a certain number of courses in a wide variety of subjects. One objective is to provide you as a student with an exposure to many areas of study. As a result, you may be better equipped to select a major area of emphasis for your life's work. Another major objective of such varied study is to help you to become a more educated and cultured person—hopefully fired with a desire to study throughout the rest of your life.

While recuperating from injuries, Cicero, one of the truly great minds and political leaders of the Roman empire, left the pressures of his governmental obligations in Rome and found opportunity for further study. He wrote:

How delightful it is to be a student again! Men should never cease from studying, from returning to those springs which so intoxicated their youth, for in books there is much wisdom and there is no end to what a man can acquire in knowledge. . . . All becomes stale and jaded that is of the body, but that which is of the mind and the spirit is never satisfied, never satiated, never exhausted. It is as if one possesses eternal youth, for one is always discovering and is always elated at some new treasure revealed to him. (As quoted in Caldwell, *A Pillar of Iron*, p. 435.)

One of your most important resolutions as a returned missionary will be to continue learning in many different areas, as we are counseled in the Doctrine and Covenants. In order to help a person become more fully educated, most good colleges and universities require that a student study more broadly than just the courses required in his or her vocational specialty. Don't make the mistake some college students do of having a negative attitude toward these general education requirements; rather, take advantage of them and let the courses add significantly to your quest to become a truly educated person. In this way you will learn how to communicate more effectively; you will better appreciate the arts, history, and various areas of science; you will become more interested in learning generally; and socially you will become much more interesting to others. And your whole life will continually be enriched from now on.

Not every job or vocation requires a college education. If your choice is to pursue a career that will not require additional college studies, you can still commit your life to being a student. For me, Albert Kohler was a choice example. He was the twelfth of thirteen children in a Swiss convert immigrant family living in Midway, Wasatch County, Utah. He grew up in dire poverty and in a family tradition that placed great emphasis upon a young person learning a trade or skill at about age twelve in order to help provide additional financial support for a large family.

In those days it was not unusual after a few years in elementary school for a young boy such as Albert, after learning some of the basics of reading, writing, and arithmetic, to drop out of school. Albert did this, and he did not intend to re-enroll. Then, one day shortly after the school year began, he met Mr. Hicks, the new teacher who had come to town. In a life-changing conversation, Mr.

Hicks asked, "Albert, are you going to be coming to school this year?"

Albert's response was, "No. No, I'm going to get a job. I'm going to learn a trade."

The teacher said, "Why don't you come for just a few days. Try it out. See how you like it." In his personal history, Albert Kohler described his experience of accepting the invitation and the teacher's personal interest in him. He went back to elementary school and was never the same again. "This teacher," as he said, "didn't answer our questions directly; but he would write on the chalkboard the names of books and places where we could go to find the answer. There I began a love for books and reading that has never left me."

I know that is true, because years later I married into his family and personally observed him. Even though Albert Kohler was a very busy, successful farmer and father of twelve children of his own (and they reared a thirteenth —a nephew), I rarely saw him inside the house without a book in his hand. His interest in reading amazed me, considering that he had only an eighth-grade education. When I gave him my first gift on the occasion of his birthday, it was a copy of William Prescott's *The Conquest of Mexico and The Conquest of Peru*—all 1,235 pages.

Albert Kohler passed away more than twenty years ago, and the book is still with the family. It no longer looks like the book I presented to him—new and crisp with pages stuck together. Rather, it is a book that has been thoroughly read—every page, every word—with some handwritten marginal notes. Where he came to a word that he did not know, it would be circled and the dictionary definition briefly sketched in the margin. He was a student. I'm confident that in his lifetime he had read much more than the average college graduate.

Mark Twain once said, "The man who does not read good books has no advantage over the man who can't read them." Fortunately for all of us in his family, Albert Kohler learned how to read, and he read.

As a nation and people, we have a long way to go to be as well educated as we ought to be. Former United States Secretary of Education William J. Bennett wrote this about the humanities, which includes many of the general education areas of study:

I would describe the humanities as the best that has been said, thought, written, and otherwise expressed about the human experience. The humanities tell us how men and women of our own and other civilizations have grappled with life's enduring, fundamental questions: What is justice? What should be loved? What deserves to be defended? What is courage? What is noble? What is base? Why do civilizations flourish? Why do they decline?

Kant defined the essence of the humanities in four questions: What can I know? What should I do? What may I hope for? What is Man? These questions are not simply diversions for intellectuals or playthings for the idle. As a result of the ways in which these questions have been answered, civilizations have emerged, nations have developed, wars have been fought, and people have lived contentedly or miserably.

If ideas are important, it surely follows that learning and life are poorer without the humanities. The humanities can contribute to an informed sense of community by enabling us to learn about and become participants in a common culture, shareholders in our civilization. But our goal should be more than just a common culture—even television and comics can give us that. We should, instead, want all students to know a common culture rooted in civilization's lasting vision, its highest shared ideals and aspirations, and its heritage. As the late philosopher Charles Frankel once said, "It is through the humanities that a civilized society talks to itself about the things that matter most."

. . . The humanities are not an educational luxury, and they are not just for (humanities) majors. They are a body of knowledge and a means of inquiry that convey serious truths, defensible judgments, and significant ideas. Properly taught, the humanities bring together the perennial questions of human life with the greatest works of history, literature, philosophy, and art. Unless the humanities are taught and studied in this way, there is little reason to offer them. The following knowledge in the humanities is essential to a college education:

Because our society is the product and we the inheritors of Western Civilization, American students need an understanding of its origins and development, from its roots in antiquity to the present. This understanding should include a grasp of the major trends in society, religion, art, literature, and politics, as well as a knowledge of the basic chronology.

A careful reading of several masterworks of English, American, and European literature.

An understanding of the most significant ideas and debates in the history of philosophy.

Demonstrable proficiency in a foreign language, and the ability to view that language as an avenue into another culture. (From "The Humanities: We Must Reclaim Our Heritage," pp. 19–20. Reproduced by kind permission of the author.)

Remember that work is, or ought to be, fulfilling. You can find jobs and careers that will help you grow and achieve new skills. Even when you find that your work is not as stimulating as you may want it to be, you can find a world of possibilities elsewhere. Read good books. Take advantage of libraries, bookstores, seminars, musicals, and other cultural events. Learn to play a musical instrument. Develop some manual skills and hobbies. One medical doctor's more enjoyable free hours are spent doing fine finish work in his woodworking shop.

A General Authority of the Church became a recognized specialist in lapidary work. He received much satisfaction from hiking in the mountains and finding choice rocks, petrified wood, and semiprecious stones. He gradually acquired the machines to cut and polish the rocks and fashion the gems that have become treasured possessions of his family and friends.

Others have taken up painting in water colors and oils and find in their hobby refreshing changes of pace. Such activities as fly-tying, fly-fishing, photography, collections of all sorts, and a thousand other possibilities can add interest and zest to your life regardless of the profession or work you choose. You can, and should, keep on learning throughout your life.

With all that you study, always remember that some truths are far more important than others. Be sure to emphasize those related to eternal truths, ordinances, and covenants along with whatever else you study.

How important is it to maintain an appropriate emphasis on spiritual learning? Note these statements from some of the wise leaders of the Church. First, from President Brigham Young:

> There are a great many branches of education: some go to college to learn languages, some to study law, some to study physic, and some to study astron-

omy, and various other branches of science. . . . But our favourite study is that branch which particularly belongs to the Elders of Israel—namely, theology. Every Elder should become a profound theologian— should understand this branch better than all the world. (In *Journal of Discourses*, 6:317.)

Next, from Elder John A. Widtsoe, who became president of two universities during his lifetime:

The man whose mind only has been trained may be likened to the ship with great engines and a huge propeller, ready to drive the ship forward, but without rudder, chart, compass, or definite destination. When we add to the man, so trained, spiritual training, then it is as if we add to the ship, with its wonderful machinery, a compass, a chart, a rudder, and a dependable intelligence which controls the whole machinery, above and below deck, so that the vessel may reach a safe haven, according to a definite purpose. (In Conference Report, October 1922, p. 48.)

It is a paradox that men will gladly devote time every day for many years to learn a science or art; yet will expect to win a knowledge of the gospel, which comprehends all sciences and arts, through perfunctory glances at books or occasional listening to sermons. The gospel should be studied more intensively than any school or college subject. They who pass opinion on the gospel without having given it intimate and careful study are not lovers of the truth, and their opinions are worthless. (*Evidences and Reconciliations*, pp. 16–17.)

And from President J. Reuben Clark, Jr., a distinguished international lawyer who served as a member of the First Presidency:

> There is spiritual learning just as there is material learning, and the one without the other is not complete; yet, speaking for myself, if I could have only one sort of learning, that which I would take would be the learning of the spirit, because in the hereafter I shall have opportunity in the eternities which are to come to get the other, and without spiritual learning here my handicaps in the hereafter would be all but overwhelming. (In Conference Report, April 1934, p. 94.)

Regardless of the college or university you may select, one overriding consideration that you dare not forget is maintaining the balance between your regular college studies and your spiritual growth and learning. If you select a Church college or university, you have assurance that the opportunities to study in formal religion classes are provided. Take advantage of them, as well as make sure that you associate with those who have really committed themselves to live up to the code of honor and the standards of the gospel which they agreed to live when they applied for admission. Unfortunately, there are a few students even at Church-sponsored colleges who do not take those commitments as seriously as they should. As a returned missionary you are in a position to help strengthen others in the areas of spiritual growth and adherence to standards as well as to maintain this appropriate balance yourself.

If you choose a college not sponsored by the Church, be sure there is an institute of religion available and enroll in a course during every term you attend. Also, take full advantage of the social contacts that are available there with those who share your standards and beliefs. Full- or part-time institutes of religion have been established adjacent to hundreds of college campuses across the nation and in many international areas. If you are not sure whether one is available near a college you are considering, contact a representative of the Church Educational System and request the information.

Many can benefit from your strength and experience as a returned missionary. You will undoubtedly have choice opportunities to share insight and testimony with many others—inside as well as outside the Church. These opportunities can provide you with some of your richest experiences of spiritual growth following your mission. All of this is possible if you do not forget to maintain the balance in your studies and learning.

There is so much more to discover about the gospel! In fact, additional gospel understanding is a search that should continue along with all the other areas of stimulating study—regardless of your career choice and throughout your entire life.

9

Maintaining the Spirit

Almost all returned missionaries know that there were times during their missions when they received special help from the Spirit. Memories were quickened, language facilities enhanced, testimonies strengthened, and discernment granted when needed.

Now that you are home, you still need the help that can come from the Spirit if you are to make the inspired decisions that lie in your future. You have never faced a time when what you decide will have a more profound influence on the rest of your life in this world and on through the eternities. What a blessing it will be if you can be assisted by the Spirit in making the best career choice for you and your future family! Also, what a strength it will be to be guided in making the most appropriate selection of an eternal companion! All of this is possible if you are close enough to the Spirit to receive personal revelation.

As you are well aware, personal revelation is one of the products and promises of being a member of The Church of Jesus Christ of Latter-day Saints. Not only is revelation a blessing that comes to prophets for the guidance of Church members throughout the world but it is also a blessing that is intended to come to every member for his or her own needs. As a group, no one should be better prepared to receive spiritual guidance than returned missionaries.

President Brigham Young said: "There is no doubt, if a person lives according to the revelations given to God's people, he may have the Spirit of the Lord to signify to him his will, and to guide and to direct him in the discharge of his duties, in his temporal as well as his spiritual exercises. I am satisfied, however, that in this respect, *we live far beneath our privileges*." (*Discourses of Brigham Young*, p. 32; italics added.)

Most missionaries indicate that they came closer to the Spirit in the mission field than at any other previous time of their lives. A regret frequently mentioned by returned missionaries is that they do not feel as close to the Spirit as they did when they were in the field. The missionary who had the Spirit in his or her work succeeded, and those who didn't, to a very great extent failed. Now that you are home, the same principle follows.

"The best thing about my mission," one Elder said, "was the Spirit I felt while I was out there. Now that I'm home, I worry that I'll lose it and things won't go so well."

One study of a group of returned missionaries revealed that maintaining the Spirit was ranked at the top of their list of concerns. Spirituality is an asset you do not want to lose, and especially now that a lot of other concerns press in on you.

Every chapter in this book contains some important and helpful counsel, but this one deals with the most important. Even if you were to follow all the other suggestions but fail to achieve success in cultivating spirituality for the rest of your life, you would indeed ultimately fail.

Spirituality is the *sine qua non* of successful living for a member of The Church of Jesus Christ of Latter-day Saints. *Sine qua non* is a Latin phrase that literally translated means, "Without which not." In other words—using our present context—you could be successful in a lot of areas. Economically you could earn a lot of money. Scholastically you could achieve high honors and receive several academic degrees and recognitions. Socially, you could mix with the best people and meet and marry the finest of individuals. As a result of marketing some talent you may have, you could literally become wealthy and world famous. Politically, you could be elected to the highest offices. You could achieve immense worldly influence and power. Regardless of what you may accomplish, however, if you do not maintain the Spirit now that you are home from your mission, you will not be successful in the eternal scheme of things, in that which matters most. In the end you will not be as happy and successful as you would like or ought to be. Spirituality is indeed the *sine qua non*. It is *absolutely essential.*

One of the most important gifts you bring home from your mission is your own increased spirituality. This special spirit is recognized by others. For example, at a family gathering, word had been received that a favorite uncle was having some health problems and had to report early in the following week to the hospital for some complicated surgical procedures. He wanted to receive a blessing. There were several Melchizedek Priesthood bearers present.

"Whom would you like to anoint and administer?"

After a brief pause, the uncle responded, "I think I would like the two recently returned missionaries to do me the favor."

He sensed the freshness of spirit and faith these young men had brought home with them from their mission experiences. A third young returned missionary was invited to offer a family prayer prior to the administration. All gathered around and witnessed the outpouring of the Spirit as the administration took place and the blessings and promises were voiced.

Without doubt, there is a special spirit that accompanies those fresh from the mission field, and missionaries hope to be able to retain it.

Fortunately, most missionaries do retain spirituality at an acceptable level, but some do not. You will come into contact with all sorts of pressures, including some from premission associates who may not share your values. Someone among a group of nonmissionary friends reportedly said, "Just give us a month and we'll have Bill right back where he was long before he left on his mission."

Occasionally, rumors are circulated indicating a high level of inactivity among returned missionaries. Don't believe them. Even though there are occasional exceptions, most continue very active in the Church and live lives consistent with the principles of the gospel after their missions. One effective and extensive research study involved a follow-up of hundreds of returned missionaries. Included in the results were the following important findings.

Respondents reported an average attendance at sacrament meeting of 83 percent and an average attendance at Priesthood or Relief Society and Sunday School of 82 percent during the 12 months prior to receiving the questionnaire. Ninety-seven percent reported attendance at sacrament meeting at least once a month, 95 percent reported attendance at at least one priesthood or Relief Society meeting per month, and 96 percent reported attendance at Sunday School at least monthly during the same period of time.

Twenty-nine percent . . . were single at the time of the survey. Of the 71 percent who were married, 95 percent had been sealed in the temple.

Eighty-five percent . . . reported that they were in possession of a current temple recommend at the time of the survey.

Ninety-two percent . . . reported that they were full tithe payers. Five percent indicated that they were part tithe payers at the time of the survey.

Ninety-seven percent . . . indicated that they observe the Word of Wisdom.

Eighty-nine percent . . . held at least one church calling, and 65 percent held two or more church callings at the time of the survey.

On a 5-point religiosity scale, with 1 representing the "not religious" end of the spectrum and 5 representing the "very religious," 89 percent . . . rated themselves as 4 or above. (Excerpts from Madsen, "Church Activity of Returned Missionaries," pp. 108, 109, 110. Reproduced by kind permission of the author.)

Those results constitute an impressive ratio of consistent activity among those who have fulfilled missions, but note that a few were lost along the way. As a returned missionary, you have joined a powerful group of well-trained and committed Church members on whose shoulders will fall a considerable measure of responsibility in the years ahead.

You will need to guard against negative pressures and influences that can destroy spirituality in your life. Decide now where you stand and what you will and will not do before the moment of temptation arrives. Elder Bowman, just after he returned from his mission, told that after a lot of persuading, he agreed to go with his friend to a dance at a public dance hall that did not have the best of reputations but attracted a lot of young adults.

Elder Bowman was nervous and chose to sit and watch. His friend came running over and said to everyone in a loud voice, "This guy wants to dance! He hasn't for so long I think he has forgotten." Soon his friend brought him a girl to dance with on a slow song. Elder Bowman said, "She snuggled up to me, put her head on my shoulder, and whispered, 'What's your name?' If my mission president had seen the situation I was in, I'd have been in deep trouble. These were the thoughts that plagued my mind. When the dance ended and I was released from her 'chains,' I felt like Joseph when he ran from Potiphar's wife. I quickly sneaked out of the door with my coat and went home, never to return." (Adapted from an article in the Ricks College *Scroll*, September 28, 1988, pp. 13–14.) Precommitment to solid decisions and directions before the time of pressure or crisis is a great help. Many decisions you will need to make only once.

President Kimball described a situation with one returned missionary who had let things slip in his life and explained some of the reasons why he had lost the spirit of his mission:

> At a distant stake conference one Sunday I was approached after the meeting by a young man whose face was familiar. He identified himself as a returned missionary whom I had met out in the world a few years ago. He said he had not attended the conference but came at its conclusion wanting to see me again. Our greetings were pleasant and revived some choice memories. I asked him about himself. He was in college, still single, and fairly miserable. I asked him about his service in the Church and the light in his eyes went out and a dull, disappointed face

fashioned itself as he said, "I am not very active in the Church now. I don't feel the same as I used to feel in the mission field. What I used to think was a testimony has become something of disillusionment. If there is a God I am not sure anymore. I must have been mistaken in my zeal and joy."

I looked him through and through and asked him some questions. . . .

The answers came as expected. He had turned loose his hold on the iron rod. He associated largely with unbelievers. He read, in addition to his college texts, works by atheists, apostates, and Bible critics. He had ceased to pray to his Heavenly Father. His communication poles were burned; his lines sagging.

I asked him now, "How many times since your mission have you read the New Testament?"

"Not any time," was the answer.

"How many times have you read the Book of Mormon through?"

The answer, "None."

"How many chapters of scripture have you read? How many verses?"

Not one single time had he opened the sacred books. He had been reading negative and critical and faith-destroying things and wondered why he could never smile. He never prayed anymore yet wondered why he felt so abandoned and so alone in a tough world. For a long time he had not partaken of the sacrament of the Lord's Supper and wondered why his spirit was dead.

Not a penny of tithing had he paid and wondered why the windows of heaven seemed closed and locked and barred. (*The Teachings of Spencer W. Kimball*, pp. 128–29.)

This missionary had failed to follow the guidelines that could have helped him maintain this priceless gift of spirituality. To help prevent you from finding yourself in a similar circumstance, here are some basic, protective guidelines by which you can preserve a high level of spirituality in your life as a returned missionary:

Commit yourself to read at least two pages of scripture daily. If you make this simple resolution and bring yourself into contact with the spirit of the scripture, you will find that inspiration will be with you more regularly. On many days, you will obviously have the time and desire to read more than two pages; and you will do much more than just nibble. Rather, you will in truth "feast upon the words of Christ." Remember that Nephi counseled that "angels speak by the power of the Holy Ghost; wherefore, they speak the words of Christ. Wherefore, I said unto you, *feast upon the words of Christ;* for behold, *the words of Christ will tell you all things what ye should do."* (2 Nephi 32:3; italics added.) Someone once said, "If you want to speak to God, then pray; and if you want God to speak to you, read the scriptures."

President Ezra Taft Benson has repeatedly and powerfully encouraged all members to study the Book of Mormon and to read something in it every day. The Book of Mormon can be a special help to the returned missionary in maintaining spirituality and a testimony of the Savior. It has been calculated that there are 3,925 references to the Savior in the pages of the Book of Mormon, using 101 varying titles of the Lord. That means that on average there is a reference to Christ in every 1.7 verses of that important scripture. (See Black, *Finding Christ Through the Book of Mormon,* pp. 16, 31.)

It is readily apparent why a living prophet would encourage us to read daily from the Book of Mormon in order to more fully "come unto Christ." Any returned missionary who fails to follow this counsel misses a powerful divine source of spirituality.

President Marion G. Romney indicated some very impressive promises to those who read from the Book of Mormon prayerfully and regularly. He said:

- "The spirit of that great book will come to permeate our homes and all who dwell therein."
- "The spirit of reverence will increase."
- "Mutual respect and consideration for each other will grow."
- "The spirit of contention will depart."
- "Parents will counsel their children in greater love and wisdom."
- "Children will be more responsive and submissive."
- "Righteousness will increase."
- "Faith, hope, and charity—the pure love of Christ—will abound in our homes and lives, bringing in their wake peace, joy, and happiness." (*Ensign,* May 1980, p. 67.)

Be the kind of example you had hoped that your investigators would be as they sought the spirit of testimony and conviction. Don't let your Church activity slip. It is easy to become careless or to spend more time than you should in visiting other wards where friends might be located. Honor the Sabbath day by attending all your meetings each Sunday. Strictly observe the Word of Wisdom without exception. Faithfully pay your tithing—a privilege you did not participate in while in the mission field.

Even though we belong to a church in which we do not seek or covet callings or position, there is nothing wrong with letting your bishop know that you sustain him and other leaders fully and that you are ready and willing to serve in *any* capacity where the bishop feels you could be of meaningful service. If you serve faithfully in your calling with all your heart, might, mind, and soul—just as the scriptures counsel—you will discover welcomed outpourings of the Spirit and of inspiration. Remember often that it really doesn't matter where we serve but rather how we serve. There is no calling in the Church that is beneath any one of us. If you magnify your calling, you will discover that it will require whatever talents you have—and then some.

Let the temple occupy a special place in your life during and after this period of adjustment. Live worthy of a temple recommend and use it regularly. If you do, your life will be in order and you will also place yourself in the setting where you can enjoy the choice spirit that prevails within those sacred walls. Plan your days so that there is a definite day and time noted when you will attend the temple. If this attendance is not planned, it is very easy to procrastinate and allow other, less spiritual activities to replace this source of spiritual nourishment.

Decide now that you will attend your Church meetings and keep the Sabbath day holy—not just during the three-hour block of scheduled meetings but throughout the rest of the day as well. Try not to miss any of the regular meetings, and carry out your assigned callings. Keeping the Sabbath day holy is not an easy suggestion to follow, because, if you are not careful, many intrusions can damage the spirit of the day. These intrusions may include, but are not limited to, such activities as professional sports and other television programming that can take a lot of time and leave you with no spiritual uplift to show for having watched it—in fact, often quite the reverse.

Always stay on the Lord's side of the line, as President George Albert Smith counseled:

My grandfather used to say to his family, "There is a line of demarcation, well defined, between the Lord's territory and the devil's. If you will stay on the Lord's side of the line you will be under his influence and will have no desire to do wrong; but if you cross to the devil's side of the line one inch, you are in the tempter's power, and if he is successful, you will not be able to think or even reason properly, because you will have lost the spirit of the Lord."

When I have been tempted sometimes to do a certain thing, I have asked myself, "Which side of the line am I on?" If I determined to be on the safe side, the Lord's side, I would do the right thing every time. So when temptation comes, think prayerfully about your problem, and the influence of the spirit of the Lord will enable you to decide wisely. There is safety for us only on the Lord's side of the line. (*Deseret News*, Church edition, June 17, 1944, p. 9; talk originally given at Utah State Agricultural College, baccalaureate address, Logan, Utah, June 4, 1944.)

If you want to be happy, remember that all happiness worthy of the name is on the Lord's side of the line and all sorrow and disappointment is on the devil's side of the line.

Keep up the Spirit by developing a constructive schedule to help take the place of the schedule you followed during your mission. One of the frequently mentioned problems faced by many returned missionaries is associated with their schedule—or lack of it. You have come from a situation in the mission field in which every major block of time of every day was outlined. You knew what you were expected to do and in which activity you should be involved. Now those guidelines are no longer there. You have other expectations but everything is less structured.

How you manage your schedule now that you are home can have a great bearing on your overall positive adjustment. It will also determine to a great extent how well you maintain the Spirit.

Give sound thought to developing a schedule and managing your time in a way that helps you achieve your objectives. Almost everyone is surprised when they discover how many hours they waste, with nothing concrete to show for their time. Many effective time management systems have been developed that could help you in this area. Focus on how you are using the hours of the day, and make sure there are very few that are not well planned.

If you are keeping your spirits at a high level, moving toward your occupational goals, and socially becoming involved in a wholesome way that will eventually lead you into a relationship that can be eternal, you can feel good about how you are using your time. On the other hand, all sorts of negative feelings can develop within you if you are idle.

One young man entered the mission field to go to Thailand immediately following his first year of college. Two years later, he arrived home on a Friday night early in June. He visited for a couple of days getting reacquainted with his family and friends and then the following Monday began a job that required a lot of vigorous physical effort, working in the forest. Fortunately, having followed mission guidelines, he had kept himself in reasonable physical condition. He wanted to earn some money for his return to college in the fall.

As valuable as the financial rewards were, of even greater importance was his having something constructive to occupy his time and thoughts immediately upon his return. Time did not weigh heavily on his hands and mind.

Missionaries who plan to wait for extended periods of time "to unwind" or "take a vacation" or to do "whatever" before becoming constructively involved in a plan to progress often have the most difficulty in readjusting and maintaining the Spirit.

Retain the enthusiasm you felt and exhibited on your best days in the mission field. President Kimball has counseled that returned missionaries should remain enthusiastic.

> If you will keep up this enthusiasm which you have here, you will be great leaders in the Church. When you see a missionary who goes home and says, "I have worked pretty hard, I shall now go home and relax," you see one on his way down. You aren't going home to relax. You are going home to raise the spirituality and activity in your wards. Someone may see you and say, "He just came back from his mission. He's radical or fanatic." Stay that way if they want to call it that. Don't let it wane or decrease.

> You are nineteen years old when you are called; maybe you will be seventy-nine when you die. In those sixty years, what a powerful influence you can bear. And you must do it! You must do it because it will be a wasted life, to a degree, if any one of you go home and let your hair grow and wear sloppy clothes and do ordinary things and break the Sabbath or any other of the laws of God.

> You see, the Lord has put you out here in the world, both the foreign and the local missionaries, not only to give the lessons, not only to bear your testimony, but to take this body and this soul of yours and make something of it. And your decision is today, not at the conclusion of your mission. It is

today and has already been made. That decision must be right, because when you get back into the swing of things the temptation will be greater. The Lord knew what he was doing when he impressed the Brethren to have you be neat and tidy and clean in the mission field. (*The Teachings of Spencer W. Kimball*, p. 592.)

Keeping yourself occupied with meaningful activities will be one of your challenges. If college is not in session, one of the best suggestions you can put into practice right now is to see that you find employment. Accept the best job available, and remember that no honorable work is beneath you.

Make a regular assessment of those basic practices in your life that can help assure that you are maintaining the Spirit. As a practical reminder and help, here is a simple checklist of ten questions that you should ask yourself regularly. Try it out. If you can honestly give an appropriate answer to each of the questions, you will more likely maintain the Spirit better than if you cannot. These ten questions are not the only ones that could be asked; you might well add some of your own, but at least include these:

1. *Do I read the scriptures daily?*
   Remember, we should "feast upon the words of Christ" and not just "nibble." (See 2 Nephi 32.)
2. *Do I really pray and not just say prayers?*
   Am I really communicating and not just repeating trite expressions? Remember, "the effectual fervent prayer of a righteous man availeth much" (James 5:16; see also Alma 34:17–27; Matthew 6:7).
3. *Is my fasting meaningful?*
   Do I do more than just get hungry? Next fast

day, focus on some particular need you have or on some other person who is in need of special blessings. (See D&C 59:13-23.)

4. *Do I go to bed early and get up early?*

"Retire to thy bed early . . . ; arise early" (D&C 88:124). President Harold B. Lee taught that more flashes of inspiration come early in the morning than at any other time of the day.

5. *Am I essentially a happy person?*

"Lift up your heart and rejoice" (D&C 31:3). "Be of good cheer" (D&C 68:6). Remember—this is a commandment and not just a suggestion.

6. *Do I work hard?*

"Thrust in your sickle with all your soul" (D&C 31:5). Have you ever met a truly spiritual person who was lazy?

7. *Am I more concerned about how rather than where I serve?*

Remember that even the Savior performed the humblest acts of service (John 13:1-17). Any calling can be accepted with a genuine willingness to serve.

8. *Do I love everyone—even enemies—and keep romantic feelings in their proper perspective?*

The Savior gave us the new commandment that we should "love one another; as I have loved you" (John 13:34-35). Don't forget how powerful at your age the temptations are to fall morally.

9. *Do I strive for unity with others as well as within myself—between my ideal and actual self?*

"Be one; and if ye are not one ye are not mine" (D&C 38:27; see also John 17:20-24). Avoid hypocrisy and recognize that there should be a oneness between a good appearance on the outside and what we really are within. You can't live two lives for long without doing yourself some real damage.

10. *Do I share my testimony with others?*

There is nothing you can do that will be any more helpful to you in maintaining the Spirit than to continue to be involved in helping non-members to become acquainted with the gospel. The Lord is pleased with us when we "open [our] mouths" and share with others the conviction we have. (See D&C 33:7-10; 60:2.)

(An expanded treatment of this topic by the author can be found in *To Grow in Spirit*, 1983.)

As mentioned, you may have other areas or questions you would like to add to the list, but if you can honestly answer these ten questions positively you will continue to be closer to the Spirit. Make it a point to review them with some regularity, because everyone's level of spirituality can change from one period to another—even in a short time. It is not uncommon for a person to experience a slump now and then, usually because one or more of these ten areas are not being followed closely.

10

Music: A Powerful Influence for Good or Ill

Music is all around you. It enters into most areas of your life. Its influence can be positive or negative. Music can help shape you one way or another. Its influence is so powerful that it merits your serious consideration now that you are home.

You have come to a level of maturity in your life that can help you evaluate wisely and make good choices. Before your mission, you probably recognized that music played an important part in your life and that some of it may have been negative.

Regarding music, the First Presidency has stated:

> Through music, man's ability to express himself extends beyond the limits of the spoken language in both subtlety and power. Music can be used to exalt

and inspire or to carry messages of degradation and destruction. It is therefore important that as Latter-day Saints we at all times apply the principles of the gospel and seek the guidance of the Spirit in selecting the music with which we surround ourselves. (Priesthood Bulletin, December 1970.)

Obviously, there is music that can build and music that can degrade. Larry Bastian, one of the accomplished musicians in the Church, wrote:

Through popular music, we have seen advocated adventures with drugs, abandonment of moral standards, resistance to authority, and inability to restrain passions and selfish desires. . . . However, it is important and heartening to note that not all popular music . . . promotes this permissive philosophy. Many popular performers consistently produce records that convey optimism and Christian moral values. (*Ensign*, April 1974, p. 37.)

In a powerful address to the youth and their leaders, Elder Boyd K. Packer has said, "There is much of today's music that [youth] may well enjoy, if they avoid the hard kind" (In Conference Report, October 1973, p. 22).

What about the "hard kind?"

"Before my mission," one Elder admitted, "I spent a lot of money and time with my tapes and records. I knew every popular recording star and the words to most of the songs. In my room, I had my own stereo and would spend a lot of time listening. When my folks complained too much about the volume, I put on my earphones and would go on listening. I attended a lot of the rock concerts that came into the area. I didn't always agree with all I saw and heard—you know, the drugs and all that went on—but I liked the music and enjoyed being with my friends. It was the 'in thing' to do. Now that I'm home, I've got to decide what to do with all this stuff."

It is true that much of rock music emphasizes drugs, sex, pornography, and rebellion. Where these influences are, the Spirit of the Lord cannot be. Some may deny it, but most who have studied the issue in depth recognize that to be the case. Excellent material has been written on the subject of the negative effects of much of popular music. (For example, read Lex de Azevedo's *Pop Music and Morality*.)

Music is everywhere and its influence is profound. Allan Bloom, a noted scholar and analyst of our whole educational society, is concerned about the negative effects of music on education. He writes:

> Though students do not have books, they most emphatically do have music. Nothing is more singular about this generation than its addiction to music. This is the age of music and the states of soul that accompany it. . . .
>
> Today, a very large proportion of young people between the ages of ten and twenty live for music. It is their passion; nothing else excites them as it does; they cannot take seriously anything alien to music. When they are in school and with their families, they are longing to plug themselves back into their music. (*The Closing of the American Mind*, p. 68. Copyright © 1987 by Allan Bloom. Reprinted by permission of Simon & Schuster, Inc.)

There are few opportunities to escape hearing it. Allan Bloom continues:

> It [music] is available twenty-four hours a day, everywhere. There is the stereo in the home, in the

car; there are concerts; there are music videos, with special channels exclusively devoted to them, on the air nonstop; there are the Walkmans so that no place —not public transportation, not the library—prevents students from communing with the Muse, even while studying. (*The Closing of the American Mind,* p. 68. See copyright detail above.)

He is very much concerned about music's effect on education:

The issue here is its effect on education, and I believe it ruins the imagination of young people and makes it very difficult for them to have a passionate relationship to the art and thought that are the substance of liberal education. (*The Closing of the American Mind,* p. 79. See copyright detail above.)

Recently, a nonmember couple came into my office. The husband had been involved in juvenile corrections work in California. They wanted to discuss their concern about the negative effects of certain music on teenagers specifically and on society generally. The husband said, "We have a sixteen-year-old daughter. This Christmas one of her cousins gave her this cassette tape recorded by one of the most popular musicians of the day. I thought I would check it before she listened to it."

He shared with me the tape, which was entitled *Faith.* All the lyrics were printed on the cover that accompanied it. When I read them, I was shocked. It was a series of lyrics explicitly advocating immoral sexual relations and drugs, and urging a rebellion against anyone who would object to such practices. Obviously, we live in a time when millions —even billions—of dollars are spent on rock music. In this era, gold is indeed being mined from "rock." Unfortunately, a good share of it undermines spirituality and many of the values we hold to be sacred.

For years, our Church leaders have issued warnings against the dangers of much of the popular rock music. At one of the general conferences several years ago, President Ezra Taft Benson read portions of a letter from a college music professor and concerned father describing the dangers of much of the day's popular music:

"Music creates atmosphere. Atmosphere creates environment. Environment influences behavior. What are the mechanics of this process?

"*Rhythm* is the most physical element in music. It is the only element in music that can exist in bodily movement without benefit of sound. A mind dulled by drugs or alcohol can still respond to the beat.

"*Loudness* adds to muddling the mind. Sound magnified to the threshold of pain is of such physical violence as to block the higher processes of thought and reason. (And turning down the volume of this destructive music does not remove the other evils.) . . .

"*Repetition* to the extreme is another primitive rock device. . . .

"*Gyrations*, a twin to rock rhythm, are such that even clean hands and a pure heart cannot misinterpret their insinuations. . . .

"*Darkness* [and dimmed lights] is another facet of the rock scene. It is a black mass that deadens the conscience in a mask of anonymity. Identity lost in darkness shrinks from the normal feelings of responsibility.

"*Strobe lights* split the darkness in blinding shafts that reduce resistance like the lights of an interrogator's third degree or the swinging pendulum of the hypnotist who would control your behavior. . . .

"The whole psychedelic design . . . is a swinging door to drugs, sex, rebellion, and Godlessness. Combined with the screaming obscenities of the lyrics, this mesmerizing music has borne the fruit of filth." (*Ensign*, December 1971, p. 53.)

In a general conference address, Elder Boyd K. Packer suggested: "I would recommend that you go through your record albums and set aside those records that promote the so-called new morality, the drug, or the hard rock culture" (*Ensign*, January 1974, p. 27).

On the positive side, there is much to be said for music. Music does have great power for good. It is considered to be the most ancient of the arts. It is mentioned in the Old Testament as early as Genesis. Jubal was referred to as "the father of all such as handle the harp and organ" (Genesis 4:21). David was one who handled the harp so well that King Saul requested that he play for him to lift his spirits. David is given credit for many of the Psalms, which were actually lyrics to songs and hymns of praise to the Lord. Many of these he would have accompanied on the harp. Before the greatest event in the history of the world, Jesus and his disciples sang a hymn together, and then he went to Gethsemane (see Matthew 26:30). Just before his martyrdom, the Prophet Joseph Smith asked Elder John Taylor to sing "A Poor Wayfaring Man of Grief" (Smith, *History of the Church*, 6:614–15.)

In his letter to the Ephesians, Paul encouraged them to "be filled with the Spirit; speaking to yourselves in psalms and hymns and spiritual songs, singing and making melody in your heart to the Lord; giving thanks always for all things unto God and the Father in the name of our Lord Jesus Christ" (Ephesians 5:18–20).

President Harold B. Lee stated at the conclusion of a general conference that in his thirty-two years as a General Authority he had learned that the most inspired preaching is always accompanied by beautiful, inspired music.

The effects of good music are illustrated by these statements:

> Music is the mediator between the spiritual and the sensual life. (Beethoven)
>
> Music washes away from the soul the dust of everyday life. (Auerbach)
>
> Music wakes the soul, and lifts it high, and wings it with sublime desires, and fits it to bespeak the Deity. (Addison)
>
> It [music] has taught men gentleness and peace, and it has led them onward to heroic deeds. Music comforts the lonely and harmonizes the discord of crowds. Music is a necessary luxury to all men. (Davenport, "It's the Language of Angels," p. 1-B.)

During the Reformation, Martin Luther was responsible for doing a great deal to promote the singing of hymns in church services. He wrote: "Music is one of the fairest and glorious gifts of God, to which Satan is a bitter enemy, for it removes from the heart the weight of sorrow, and the fascination of evil thoughts."

According to J. Edgar Hoover, past director of the FBI, involvement with good music and training has beneficial effects on young people: "The child who receives music training, and who finds joy in singing and making music, will not make mischief. The girl who sings and plays the piano does not pick your pocket. The boy who sings and draws the violin bow, is not the boy who draws the gun." (Cited in Davenport, "It's the Language of Angels," p. 1-B.)

While serving your mission, you probably came to appreciate the uplifting influence of the hymns in your own life as well as in that of your companions and investigators.

One Elder admitted, "When I was home, I didn't sing much in the ward during the congregational singing. When I arrived at the MTC, I made a discovery. I don't know when I have been more inspired and motivated than when about two thousand missionaries stood and sang 'Ye Elders of Israel' or 'Called to Serve.' When I really concentrated on the words in 'More Holiness Give Me,' something special happened within me. Just singing it made me want to try harder to do what I knew I should. On my mission, I knew that I needed all the help from the Lord I could get, and one of my favorite hymns came to be, 'I Need Thee Every Hour.' "

You may have had some similar experience during your mission. You may have come to understand why the Lord said, "For my soul delighteth in the song of the heart; yea, the song of the righteous is a prayer unto me, and it shall be answered with a blessing upon their heads" (D&C 25:11–12).

I agree with Lex de Azevedo, who wrote:

> Music is clearly one of the great and holy gifts which our Father has given us for our blessing and joy. Satan, according to his nature, has labored to twist and corrupt this instrument of joy into an instrument of death. It is always his work to spoil that which is finest and trick us into turning our life-giving powers against ourselves. But though Satan can tempt us to misuse this gift, its power for good remains and will remain forever.
>
> Music, the royal art medium of the emotions, sometimes gives expression to those deep feelings

better than words. Spoken hallelujahs can never compare with those hallelujahs sung in the glorious chorus of Handel's *Messiah.* The emotional impact of the audience as it rises to its feet cannot be expressed in words. It can only be experienced.

After words are spoken and written, printed and typed, and our hearts still yearn to express more, it is then that music rises to fill the measure of its creation. (*Pop Music and Morality,* p. 120.)

Now it is your choice to decide how you will let music affect you. If you choose wisely, your adjustment to life generally will be much more successful.

11

Don't Forget the Physical

After being in the mission field for thirty-one months, I returned to the farm just in time for the beginning of the first crop of the hay season. It seemed as though the bales had gained weight. It didn't take long to discover that everyone else on our crew was in much better physical condition than I was. I was frustrated and depressed. I felt I did not measure up. Adjusting physically to being home on the farm was not easy. Back in those days, fitness programs had not yet been developed to help missionaries stay in condition.

The physical adjustment that comes to many as they return from their missions presents some challenges. If you have followed the suggestions of Church leaders—the General Authorities as well as those in the mission field—you have maintained an exercise regimen that has helped you.

I hope that is your situation now. In any case, you will always need to give careful attention to this important area of your life. Good physical conditioning requires the development of excellent habits. About habit, an unidentified author has written:

I am your constant companion. I am your greatest helper or your heaviest burden. I will push you onward or drag you down to failure. I am completely at your command. Half the things you do you might just as well turn over to me, and I will be able to do them quickly and correctly. I am easily managed. You must merely be firm with me. Show me exactly how you want something done, and after a few lessons, I will do it automatically. I am the servant of all great men, and alas, of all failures, as well. Those who are great, I have made great. Those who are failures, I have made failures. I am not a machine, though I work with all the precision of a machine, plus the intelligence of a man. You may run me for profit, or run me for ruin, it makes no difference to me. Take me, train me, be firm with me, and I will place the world at your feet. Be easy with me and I will destroy you. Who am I? I am habit.

In previous chapters we have discussed your responsibilities to continually progress in spiritual, intellectual, and social segments of your life. This book would not be complete without some direct reference to your needs and responsibilities in this vital physical area—including maintaining your health.

Remember that Jesus increased not only in wisdom and favor with God and man but also in stature (see Luke 2:52). He developed physically, and obviously had the strength and stamina to carry out an arduous ministry that

included long hours and walking many miles through difficult terrain and adverse travel conditions.

You need at this time of your life to make sure that you
are doing everything you can to assure that you will have
the physical health, strength, and stamina needed to accomplish all that lies ahead of you. With health, almost
everything is possible; without it, our handicaps are immense. Unfortunately, when we are feeling well, we think
little about our health; but when something seriously goes
wrong, we have a hard time thinking about anything else.

A huge quantity of written information is available in
books and magazines on the subject of maintaining health.
In America today this has become one of the items of great
public concern, particularly among those who are a bit
older than the average recently returned missionary. With
many, it has become almost an obsession. You would do
well to read, think, and make some decisions that will
assure that you continue to maintain your physical health.
For our purposes now, consider three major areas: adequate nutrition, exercise, and rest.

First, consider the area of nutrition. In this era of fast
food establishments, soft drinks, and what many call "junk
foods," a significant proportion of young people apparently
consider a balanced diet for almost any meal to be a candy
bar or pastry in one hand and a soft drink in the other. If
this is your style, you will need to "repent."

Much is written about the effects of inappropriate
cholesterol levels in the blood stream or inadequate fiber in
the diet. Articles appear regularly about the role of appropriate levels of vitamins, minerals, and proteins. There is
much more to sort through than you will likely have time
or, in some cases, interest to do. You will do well to emphasize, along with everything else on your menu, such items
as fresh vegetables, fruits, and whole grains in goodly proportion.

During your mission you probably shared verses from the Word of Wisdom with your investigators countless times. Now that you are home, try an experiment. Turn to the Doctrine and Covenants and reread section 89 with your own health in mind. The positive counsel given regarding nutrition and health is phenomenal, and we have had it in the Church since 1833! The Word of Wisdom is certainly one of the obvious evidences of the validity of the Prophet Joseph Smith's mission and teachings. Note these excerpts:

All wholesome herbs God hath ordained for the constitution, nature, and use of man—

Every herb [including vegetables] in the season thereof, and every fruit in the season thereof; all these to be used with prudence and thanksgiving.

Yea, flesh also of beasts and of the fowls of the air. . . . are to be used sparingly. . . .

All grain is ordained for the use of man . . . to be the staff of life. . . .

All grain is good for the food of man; as also the fruit of the vine; that which yieldeth fruit, whether in the ground or above the ground—

Nevertheless, wheat for man. . . .

And all saints [and that certainly includes returned missionaries] who remember to keep and do these sayings, walking in obedience to the commandments, shall receive health in their navel and marrow to their bones;

And shall find wisdom and great treasures of knowledge, even hidden treasures;

And shall run and not be weary, and shall walk and not faint.

And I, the Lord, give unto them a promise that

the destroying angel shall pass by them, as the children of Israel, and not slay them. (D&C 89:10–12, 14, 16–21.)

Every promise seems especially tailored to meet the needs of a returned missionary! Follow the counsel, and the blessings will surely be yours.

Next, consider your exercise program. Decide now that you will include in your life a regular, appropriate, and adequate exercise program that will meet the needs of stimulating sufficient heart rate, circulation, and large muscle development and tone at levels that for you will be health-producing. Remember what was said about the power and nature of habits, and then work to establish those that will be best for you.

Choose your sport or exercise—jogging, walking (considered by many to be even superior to running), cycling, racquetball, or whatever you think meets your needs—and then do it daily, or at least three times a week.

Some have said that it takes at least three weeks—twenty-one consecutive days—to establish a habit. If you have any questions about your physical condition and your chosen activity, get a competent medical opinion. Even when you feel pressure to be doing other things, be consistent with your exercise program and you will more likely have the physical vitality to accomplish those other goals and tasks.

Determine what your optimum weight level is and then work diligently to maintain it. As you get older, you may have the experience one returned missionary described: "When I got home from my mission, I weighed about 137 pounds. Regardless of how much I ate, for the next seventeen years I didn't vary more than a pound or two in either direction. After I hit the early forties, things changed. Everything started centering around my waist, and I put on more than thirty pounds. Obviously, I want to get a lot of it off, and that takes a lot of will power."

Again, habit and self-discipline have a lot to do with any success in this area. Make up your mind to keep your weight under control through sufficient exercise and nutritious eating. One Elder reported, "The most important exercise I do is to push myself away from the table and all the fattening goodies that are there."

One of your most motivational decisions could be to exercise with others who have similar commitments to health and regular physical activity. One returned missionary finds it's easier to have a regular schedule with friends. "We have our group that goes down to the gym three nights a week after we have finished studying and get a good sweat up with an hour of fast basketball. I know I feel better with the exercise, and getting to sleep is no problem at all."

Others find the early morning to be the best time for them. Decide which is best for you, exercise regularly, and all the benefits will come to you.

The third important area to help you maintain good physical condition is getting adequate rest—not too much nor too little. The daily schedule you were expected to follow in the mission field was based on some important eternal truths and not on just some disciplinary procedure someone had concocted to make life difficult. You were expected to be in bed at a reasonable time, get adequate rest, and then be up early in the morning ready to face the day with vigor. It is a good feeling to know that you have begun your day by overcoming the desire to stay in bed. If you have had adequate rest, you can then move on to conquer many more obstacles during the day. As you have likely heard, in this area it is a matter of "mind over mattress."

Remember the scripture: "Cease to be idle; cease to be unclean; cease to find fault one with another; *cease to sleep longer than is needful; retire to thy bed early, that ye may not be weary; arise early, that your bodies and your minds may be invigorated"* (D&C 88:124; italics added).

Some returned missionaries get back into habits of going to bed too late. Often it is television viewing or midweek dating that robs them of an earlier time for rest. When you go to bed later than you should, you are not rested during those early quiet hours when your productivity should be high. As a result, you may find yourself to be like some college students who habitually (there's that reference to habit again!) stay in bed just as long as they can and then rush hectically to class as near its beginning as possible. These late risers are thus running behind and partially defeated right from the day's beginning. They often find it necessary to stay up later at night to try to catch up, then, like a revolving door, the next day they are back into the same problem.

Scientific research supports the idea that there is an optimum amount of sleep for each individual and that too much or too little can reduce one's efficiency. One study in California contained the information that "people who had 7 to 8 hours of sleep were healthier than those who slept 6 hours or less and those who slept 9 hours or more" (as reported in *Ensign*, January 1981, p. 11).

Those who remember the importance of physical conditioning and act accordingly get adequate rest, sufficient exercise, and wholesome nutrition. They grow in stature and have the physical strength and stamina to accomplish their important goals.

12

Especially for Returned Sister Missionaries

The first returned missionary I ever met was a Sister missionary. She was my Aunt Sarah, one of my mother's younger sisters. Near the beginning of the 1930s, when as a result of the Depression there were very few full-time missionaries serving, Aunt Sarah responded to a call. Her father, my grandfather, was serving as her bishop at the time. She went to the Western States Mission, with Denver, Colorado, as her mission headquarters. It seemed to me as if she had gone to the end of the world. Some of my earliest memories were associated with the excitement the family shared each time we received one of her letters from the mission field.

The day finally arrived when she returned home to our small farming community of Banida, Idaho. We made the trip to Coulam, about two miles away, where there was a train stop. Almost all of the family were there, along with most of the ward members from our little town. We waited and strained our eyes and ears for the first sign of the approaching train. It was exciting to look down the track and just barely see the smoke and the growing speck of an engine coming to bring my aunt home. I remember so well how beautiful she looked to me. When she got off the train with all of her luggage, there were a lot of hugs, kisses, and excitement; and it was then that my desire to go on a mission became more firmly entrenched in my mind. I became even more convinced later on when she reported her mission and told us of some of the spiritual experiences she had had. I was six years old at the time.

A few years later, the somber shadows of World War II came with all of its pressures, problems, injuries, and death, which had their profound influence in our own small area. No missionaries were called from our community during that period of time. Little did I realize that my call to go to Mexico and Central America would be the next full-time mission call to come to our ward. To this day, I am grateful for the example of that Sister missionary whose service had such a powerful impact on me. Consequently, I write this chapter with some deep feelings of appreciation for this special group of missionaries.

To be a returned missionary is an accomplishment of great significance. Every young man who completes a mission has fulfilled an important priesthood *obligation*. Every young woman who fulfills a mission has taken advantage of a great *opportunity* to respond to her call from the prophet of the Lord to help with the overall Church responsibility to preach the gospel to the world.

As far back as the 1930s, the First Presidency commended the service of Sister missionaries: "It is estimated that more than sixty thousand members of the Church have served in the mission field since its organization. . . . Greatly to our advantage, we have included women as well as men in our missionary system." (*Millennial Star,* 27 July 1933, p. 337.)

Elder Franklin D. Richards, writing a message to young women, said:

> My experience has indicated that sister missionaries are as effective as elders in leading people to baptism and that a mission gives a woman as much benefit in her later life as it does to an elder. She becomes a better wife, a better mother, a better Relief Society president—just better in every way.
>
> So, a mission is a worthy goal for any young Latter-day Saint to aspire toward. (*New Era,* January 1978, p. 4.)

While I was presiding over the Mexico City Mission, my wife and I learned that some of the most effective gospel teaching is accomplished by Sister missionaries. During one month's time, one pair of Sisters had thirty-six converts baptized into the Church. As far as we knew, that had not been accomplished by any pair of missionaries in that mission up to that time.

Elder William R. Bradford spoke of the blessings that can come to Sister missionaries when he said: "Perhaps you would also like to, and should, serve as a missionary. Many lady missionaries are now serving. The same blessings promised to young men are extended to you. Although your most important role in this life is motherhood, it may be appropriate for you to serve a mission first." (In Conference Report, October 1981, p. 72.)

One returned Sister missionary confided: "I'm so glad I went. The experiences I had in the mission field and the opportunities for service and growth were fantastic. Now that I am home, I want to get on with my life. I have worried a little about whether I'll still be able to find someone who will be right for me to marry. That is, of course, one of my life's goals. I need to decide now about where to settle. Should I go to work, to school, or what?"

As a returned Sister missionary, you are more than special: you are *very* special. You have gone beyond the call of mere duty. You have fulfilled your opportunity for service in the Lord's cause and have received the incalculable benefits that come from your personal experience in that "University of the Lord." Your life of service to members and nonmembers will be enhanced forever. You are far better trained and equipped to fulfill all of life's obligations than if you had not gone on a mission. You will have more confidence in magnifying your callings within the Church. You will feel much more comfortable in using the scriptures in every setting for as long as you live.

As a result of contacting and teaching investigators of all varieties, you have had more experience in communicating with others than you otherwise would have had. You know the doctrines of the gospel much better than you would have learned them had you not served. The scriptures will be a much greater part of your life because of the extra hours of exposure, study, and use of these sacred works in your preparation and teaching. From now on, you can enjoy the personal satisfaction of knowing that you also have received that special title and recognition of being a "returned missionary" and that you were called by the same prophetic authority as are all missionaries. You are fully entitled to a great feeling of satisfaction for what you have accomplished.

One Church leader said: "I will always be grateful for having the special opportunity of marrying a returned lady missionary. I have witnessed what that has meant in my life and also in hers. I know what it has meant in our marriage, in our home, in her opportunities to serve in and out of the Church, with our children, and now with our grandchildren. The benefits are tremendous."

All of this does not mean that there are not readjustments that need to be made in the lives of Sisters when they return from their missions. It will help your adjustment if you get into school or some other constructive activity as quickly as you can.

As with returning young men, many of life's greatest decisions lie ahead of you. Your service as a missionary and your greater understanding of the gospel have likely enhanced your realization of the importance of good homes and family life. You probably are hoping to find the right person to marry and be a partner with in creating your own home, having your own children, and even helping them to become future missionaries.

Fortunately, your mission will have helped you to become a better candidate for marriage. Your improved skills in relating to others will not go unnoticed. You have benefited from learning to adjust to a variety of personalities among your companions, the Elders who presided locally over the missionary activities, and other mission leaders. All this experience can be helpful to you in adjusting to an eternal companion and to the varied challenges that come with the process of making a successful marriage and home. In all probability, your future marriage and family life will be greatly enhanced as a result of your missionary service.

Now that you are home, it is important that you move forward with your life. However, be patient and don't feel that you must rush into any major decisions too quickly. Time is still on your side. If you haven't finished your education or training in marketable skills needed to earn a good living, move forward as quickly as possible and get that preparation behind you. It will always be a blessing, whether you marry sooner or later. A husband and father whose wife is a returned missionary said: "Even though my wife is not working outside our home, just knowing that she has her degree and is prepared to assume more responsibility if I were not around is a great source of peace of mind for me. Meanwhile, with that background of preparation, her positive influence on our children—and especially our daughters—is incalculable. They all want to go on to college as well. They want to be just as prepared as their mom. What a blessing!"

While my wife and I were serving at the Missionary Training Center, the results of a simple survey indicated that of a sample of a hundred missionaries whose mothers had served missions, a much higher percentage of all the children who were of age to serve missions had served than from a similar-sized group of a hundred missionaries whose mothers had not served a mission. With few exceptions, the returned missionary mothers had married husbands who also had served missions. Together they apparently had a great influence in their homes and on the lives of their children as far as missionary work is concerned. It is safe to say that there are few sons who grow up in homes where both parents are returned missionaries who do not choose to serve missions themselves. They experience a missionary spirit in their home from the time they are born. The families of the returned missionary mothers in this particular sample also had a higher percentage of daughters choose to serve missions. There is a strong indication that the missionary example and spirit are contagious.

Some young women return from their missions and seek employment immediately without thinking a great deal about the social contacts and possibilities available in their geographical location. This is a time to be as "wise as serpents and [gentle] as doves." Think it through. Decide where your best opportunities are for good social contacts and, if possible, locate in that area.

One highly placed Church leader counseled a single sister who was a teacher by saying: "If you are not finding anyone who looks like a good prospect for marriage in the area in which you are now working, then I suggest you move. Move to someplace where there are more prospects. It may not be the comfortable thing to do, but take advantage of the possibility while time is still on your side."

As an educated returned missionary, you have a lot more to bring to a marriage than you would otherwise have. Also, being enrolled in an educational setting can place you in a social environment where meeting marriageable prospects is more likely than if you are living and working in an area where they are few and far between.

You needn't be overly aggressive. Be patient and concentrate on preparing yourself, serving others, magnifying your callings within the Church, taking advantage of temple service opportunities, reading good books, keeping yourself in top physical condition, and reaching out to those who need your assistance, whether older or younger. During this time, don't forget to share the gospel. As the Savior taught, if you lose yourself in his service you will find yourself—find yourself more fulfilled and satisfied. If you are doing all these things, the great probability is that in due time someone very special will find you.

President Kimball has given some good advice to all of us:

> You need to evaluate yourselves carefully. Take a careful inventory of your habits, your speech, your appearance, your weight, and your eccentricities, if you have any. Take each item and analyze it. Can you make some sacrifices to be acceptable? You must be the judge.

Are you too talkative? Too withdrawn? Too quiet? If so, then school your thoughts and your expressions. . . .

Is your dress too old-fashioned, or too revealing, or too extreme? Are you too demanding? Do you have any eccentricities in speech, in tone, in subject matter? Do you laugh too loudly? Are you too demonstrative? Do you overdo? Are you selfish? Are you honorable in all things? . . .

Have you made yourself attractive physically—well groomed, well dressed—and attractive mentally—engaging, interesting? Are you well read? If not, then change yourself. . . .

Continue to make yourself attractive, physically, mentally, spiritually, emotionally." (*New Era*, September 1974, p. 7.)

One young returned missionary summed it up well when she said, "Up till now it hasn't worked out as far as finding the best husband for me is concerned; but meanwhile, every day of my life is blessed for having served a mission. The scriptures have come alive and are a much greater part of my daily life. I enjoy opportunities to serve in the Church. I have a lot more confidence than I used to have. Conversing about the gospel with others who are not members of the Church is now a rewarding experience rather than a frightening one. Going to the temple regularly adds an important dimension to my life, and I enjoy the people I meet there. I have a whole host of additional people to think about among the converts and other members in the mission field. They are like family. I still correspond with several of them.

"Some of my former companions are among my closest friends, and it seems as if I've known them all my life. I've decided to take each day as it comes, knowing that sooner or later everything will work out for the best, if I make each day count in a positive way. At the end of the day, I like to feel that I have made some progress toward the achievement of worthwhile goals that I came to recognize more clearly while in the mission field. For me, everything is better as a result of those eighteen months I served."

Remember, Sisters, you are more than special for having served a mission. You are *very special.*

13

If You Learned a Second Language

About 40 percent of all LDS missionaries are called to serve in parts of the world where they must learn to speak a second language. You missionaries who received these assignments had the special challenge of sharing the gospel in words and phrases which were probably unknown to you prior to your call. The language skills you have developed can become an important asset to you if you take full advantage of them. Unfortunately, some missionaries return and let their language capabilities deteriorate much more than they should.

For the sake of the Church and opportunities to serve which may come to you, you should make sure that you do not lose these skills. At some future time you may be called to serve with your spouse as a senior missionary in helping to strengthen the Church in an area of the world that speaks your particular language. Meanwhile you will be able to share with your children some of the excitement that comes from understanding and speaking a foreign language.

President Spencer W. Kimball urged returned missionaries to retain their language skills. He said: "As I spoke to these missionaries, I urged them to learn the language well and for permanence to perfect their speech and their understanding, to retain their acquired facility when they came home and even teach them to their wives and children. Tomorrow we may need them, and their sons and daughters, to teach the gospel through radio, television, and other inventions." (*The Teachings of Spencer W. Kimball,* p. 591.)

In addition to Church and family benefits, there are some important personal and national advantages that come through exposure to another culture and language. Arthur Henry King, a noted linguist, has said that "we don't know our own language until we know at least one other" (*The Abundance of the Heart,* p. 241). Your study of another language has undoubtedly given you some insights into your own language and the importance of learning to use it correctly.

As a Church and as a nation, in the area of our study of foreign languages there is an urgency that only a few have recognized. Joseph Lurie, vice president of American Field Service International, compiled a series of statements which indicate that as a nation we have a long way to go in language study:

America's young face a set of new national and international circumstances about which they have only the faintest of notions. They are, globally speaking, blind, deaf and dumb; and thus handicapped, they will soon determine the future directions of this nation. (Editorial — *Change Magazine,* October 1978.)

Increasingly U.S. foreign policy decisions must reflect a greater sensitivity to foreign cultures, to foreign public opinions, perceptions and priorities. (United States Advisory Commission on Public Diplomacy Report 1980.)

Our linguistic parochialism has had a negative effect on our trade balance. In fact, it is one of the most subtle nontariff barriers to our export expansion. . . . America does not export enough, 6–8 percent of our GNP [Gross National Product] as opposed to 15–25 percent of the GNP's of Germany and Japan. . . . Part of the reason the Japanese and the Germans sell so effectively is that they have gone to the trouble of learning about us and adapting the products they export to our tastes and markets. An impressive number of their businessmen have learned our language, and foreign business students usually have international studies as part of the curriculum. . . . (Frank A. Weil, Former Assistant Secretary of Commerce for Industry and Trade.)

The United States continues to be the only country in the world where you can graduate from college without having had one year of a foreign language prior to and during the university years. (Congressman Paul Simon, *The Tongue Tied American,* 1980.)

Most area specialist officers in the Executive Branch, including the intelligence services, do not and usually cannot, read the materials of greatest concern to them in the original and cannot converse with their foreign counterparts beyond pleasantries in the other language. (*The Tongue Tied American.*)

The State Department no longer requires any background in another language as a condition of entry into the Foreign Service. (*The Tongue Tied American.*)

In the European Division of the Office of the Secretary of Defense, there are 70–80 employees, largely dealing with base site negotiations. None of the staff speaks German or French (Allen Kassof, Executive Director, National Council on Foreign Language and International Studies.)

Of the 11 million U.S. students seeking graduate and undergraduate degrees, fewer than 1 percent are studying the languages used by three-quarters of the world's population. (*The Tongue Tied American.*)

In a recent UNESCO education study of 30,000 ten- and fourteen-year-olds in nine countries, *American students ranked next to the bottom in their comprehension of foreign cultures.* (Fred Hechinger, *The New York Times,* March 13, 1979.)

(The preceding excerpts were taken from Joseph Lurie, comp., "America . . . Globally Blind, Deaf and Dumb," *Foreign Language Annals* 15 (1982): 413–15. Reprinted with permission from the American Council on the Teaching of Foreign Languages, publishers of *Foreign Language Annals.*)

In a newspaper article, a Mr. Pfeiffer, chairman of IBM World Trade Americas-Far East Corporation, cited statistics that 4,300 of 6,000 Japanese businessmen in this country speak English, while fewer than 100 of the 10,000 Americans working in Japan know that language. That is one reason why the hundreds of Japanese-speaking returned missionaries attending Brigham Young University are considered by many observers to be a valuable national economic resource.

As a Church we probably fail to recognize fully the immense value that comes from learning a language while living in another culture. One of the impressive strengths of our current missionary program is that it takes so many thousands of young adults for extended periods into countries around the entire free world. It amazes some that at a two-year college such as Ricks—tucked away in a relatively unpopulated area of the Upper Snake River Valley in Idaho—there are so many hundreds of students who have lived in dozens of countries throughout the free world and who collectively speak more than thirty languages. It makes the setting anything but provincial, thanks to the specialized training the missionaries experience.

Nevertheless we have yet a long way to go, since only about four out of ten missionaries are called to a second-language mission. Considering the ratio of Church members who currently serve missions, only one in six members of the Church is called to learn a second language.

Be sure that you take advantage of the college credit that most universities will grant upon demonstration of second-language abilities. In some settings, such as Brigham Young University and Ricks College, a student may acquire a significant number of credits by taking a language proficiency examination and fulfilling the prescribed procedures. In many colleges you can receive credits equal to the equivalent of more than a semester of college study. At the cost of university credits these days, that is an important extra asset that should not be overlooked. It will be better for you to take the examination as soon as you can following your mission while your spoken language skills are still at their peak.

If you have studied one of the languages offered in the college you may be attending now that you are home, it would be advantageous, even if you do not plan to be a language major, to take an advanced course that will sharpen your grammar and composition skills in the language and thus help you maintain your abilities in the language at a higher level than you likely would otherwise achieve in the years ahead.

Now, what does becoming acquainted with a foreign language mean at a personal level? I was called to serve a mission forty years ago. I had studied Spanish for two years in high school and for another year at the college level before being called to serve as a missionary in Mexico and Central America, long before the Missionary Training Center existed. I knew upon arrival that I did not know the language well enough to accomplish adequately what I had been called to do, but living in the countries was an immense help. And it was not just the language that I became acquainted with—it was also the culture and, especially, the people. The Mexicans and Costa Ricans still occupy a special place in my heart, as do all people who share that language and heritage. For that blessing I will always be grateful.

After returning from that thirty-one-month mission experience, I found in advanced courses in Spanish grammar and composition at BYU a deeper love for the language that lives with me to this day—thanks to my professors. I discovered that there is, in fact, power and melody in Spanish poetry. I love these lines from the Central American poet Ruben Dario (if you understand Spanish, the message will be clear; and even if you don't understand Spanish, if you were to hear the poem pronounced you could listen for the music in the language itself):

> Juventud, divino tesoro
> Ya te vas para no volver
> Cuando quiero llorar, no lloro
> Y, a veces, lloro sin querer.

My personal, nonliterary translation of this is:

> Youth, divine treasure.
> You are now leaving never to return.
> When I want to cry, I don't;
> And, sometimes, when I do not want to, I cry.

I have appreciated so much coming into contact with the literary masterpiece *Don Quixote de la Mancha* by Miguel de Cervantes. I certainly do not claim to be a literary authority in Spanish, but I did come to recognize that, for me, Cervantes is to Spanish what Shakespeare is to English. In that monumental work, we read of Don Quixote's theological discussion with Sancho Panza; and after all of Don Quixote's fiery speech and conversation on the idealism in man, Sancho's response was to yawn and say, "Bien predica quien bien vive, y yo no sé otras teologías" (part 2, chapter 20), which translated is, "He preaches well who lives well, and I know no more theology than that."

For me, that has become an important lesson because, in the final analysis, what we know of languages will not make a great deal of difference unless we become better persons and thus better examples. In the end, it would be marvelous if we all could agree that "he preaches well who lives well," and even without a Latter-day Saint's opportunities to know a lot more theology than that, one could still live a very productive life.

As a returned missionary who has learned another language, you have acquired a great asset that can enrich your life. You should not lose it. Make it a point to read and speak it regularly. Find others, especially native speakers or other returned missionaries, who share the language and practice it. Read aloud a few verses from the Book of Mormon each day in your mission language so that your tongue and ear retain their capacity. When you are married, take advantage of teaching your spouse and children some of the language so they will appreciate it and provide you with additional opportunities to keep in practice.

You cannot know at this time all the opportunities that lie ahead of you to use the language you have learned. Examples come to the surface at the least expected times.

Two friends of mine decided to become partners in a retail franchising business. In order to be successful, it was necessary for them to locate a good position in a new shopping mall. When they inquired about the availability of space for rent, they were informed that there was none available and a long waiting list of applicants for space had accumulated. It seemed that there was little chance to make the arrangements they felt were so important to their venture.

The manager of the mall was noted for being a hardheaded and sometimes gruff businessman. The partners decided to go and visit personally with him anyway. In the course of their conversation they were told that no space was available for their business at that time. Incidentally, in their conversation, they learned that the manager had been born in Norway. At that point, Glen, who coincidentally had served his mission there, began to speak to the manager in his native tongue. The whole situation changed. The manager warmed up and was not nearly so stern as he had at first seemed. In the end he said, "You know, I like the description of your business. We will see that you get a choice location as soon as you are ready to start."

If for no other reason, you should keep up your language skills because there may be those you will meet in the future who will be brought to a knowledge of the gospel and the meaning of life as a result of your being able to explain some principles of truth in their native tongue.

While on a flight to Hawaii, my wife and I noted that seated across the aisle was a family consisting of a husband, wife, and two young daughters. It was going to be a long flight, and we and others around us were annoyed when the wife started to smoke in our nonsmoking section of the plane. I determined that she must be a very insensitive person.

The stewardess promptly invited her to stop smoking

and she quickly responded. We soon noted that they were obviously speaking Spanish. I had noted that when the stewardess had come to serve them, they did not speak English. I decided that the least I could do would be to greet them and find out if there was anything I could do to be of service. I walked up the aisle, around the bulkhead, through the serving area and passageway, and down the other side so that I could pass by the oldest of the two daughters, who was seated on the center aisle. When I caught her attention and greeted her in English, she shook her head and turned to her father seated next to her. He also shook his head and managed to say in a very pronounced accent, "We no speak'a Angleesh."

At that point I drew on Spanish I had learned forty years before while serving my first mission to Mexico and asked them how they were enjoying their trip. Here a minor miracle occurred. Their faces brightened up. The husband turned to his wife, and she also joined in. When I heard that they were from Mendoza, Argentina, I was able to say that I had been to Argentina several times, although not to Mendoza. I mentioned that I had also been to Santiago, Chile, and at that point Mrs. Rivera almost jumped out of her seat with enthusiasm. *"¡Yo soy chilena!* [I am Chilean!]" They were even more animated.

We had a choice visit, during which I was able to help them with some information they needed to know about their trip to Hawaii. I mentioned the Polynesian Cultural Center as being a "must" on their agenda in order to help them understand the various peoples of the South Pacific, and it was natural to mention the students from the Brigham Young University–Hawaii campus who work and perform there. They also wanted to know more about the church that sponsored Ricks College, where we were serving. We felt that we had some delightful new-found friends, and they were given the privilege of knowing a little more about the restored Church.

It continues to be impressive to me how many times some knowledge of a language comes in handy. Once Barbara and I boarded a plane in Luxor, Egypt, along with our touring group of members of the Church. We were located near the rear of the plane. Shortly after being seated, Barbara leaned over and whispered, "Joe, I think that couple up there [a few rows in front of us] are speaking Spanish. Why don't you trade places with the brother from our group who is seated across the aisle and find out where they are from."

As soon as the plane was airborne, I made my way up the aisle, traded places with my friend, and then began a conversation with the couple. I discovered that they were a medical doctor and his wife from Mexico City on a private vacation tour of Egypt and the Near East. In all the visits we had made to Egypt, this was the first time we had met any tourist there from Mexico.

"Oh, you are from Mexico City and a medical doctor."

"Yes. I am a surgeon."

"I have a friend from the United States who is now living in Mexico City who is also a medical doctor. He is a specialist in internal medicine. Perhaps you would like to become acquainted with him."

He said that he would be very much interested. At that particular point, I did not mention that my friend was Dr. Quinton S. Harris, who had been my missionary companion almost forty years before and who was then serving as president of the Mexico City North Mission.

Dr. Cervantes gave me his name and address, and I later mailed the information on to Mexico City. Not long after, we received a letter from President Harris describing some unusual circumstances—especially considering the millions of people and thousands of surgeons who are located in Mexico City. Here is a portion of the letter:

Dear Joe and Barbara,

What a coincidence receiving your letter with the news about Dr. and Mrs. Cervantes! (Or was it just a coincidence?) I had a missionary who became ill last week and needed an operation. I had my secretary set up an appointment with the surgeon. The appointment was the day before your letter arrived.

The surgeon had seen another missionary for us some time ago, but I had never met him. This time I went with the missionary, because I wanted to get acquainted with the doctor. He was trained at the Washington, D. C., General Hospital and Georgetown University, was Board Certified in Surgery, etc. We had a nice chat. Surgery was scheduled for the next day in the hospital.

I stopped by the office to pick up my mail, etc., while the surgery was going on and then went back to the hospital and again visited with the surgeon regarding the operation. I hadn't opened your letter yet, though I had it in my pocket.

When I opened your letter and learned about Dr. Cervantes' experience with you, I made it a point the next morning when we went back to pick up the missionary to mention to him that I had received a note from you. He was very happy to make that connection. He has invited Ruth and me to his home tomorrow, along with some other physicians. We will see what we can do.

I'm sure you enjoyed your trip. He was impressed with the entire group he was with. We'll let you know how it turns out. Thanks for the referral and send us some more. Saludos to Barbara.

Sincerely,

Quinton S. Harris, President

In all probability that experience would not have happened without some use of a second language. Keeping up on your language skills will provide you with additional opportunities to share the gospel. You will thus be able to assist in achieving the immense challenge given by the Lord through the Prophet Joseph Smith: "For it shall come to pass in that day, that every man shall hear the fulness of the gospel in his own tongue, and in his own language" (D&C 90:11).

14

Service to Others—
An Ongoing Goal

A returned missionary made this observation: "One of the great satisfactions of my mission was to be in the service of others most of my waking hours. When I came home I discovered that I needed to adjust to the reality that much of my time and effort needed to be centered on myself and preparation for life, but I soon learned that if I wasn't careful I would overlook my responsibility to others. Just plain, down-to-earth service to those in need was one of the most important helps to me in making an adjustment to being home. I know I didn't do all I could have, but every time I made an effort to be of service to others, things went better for me."

President Kimball has said:

One has hardly proved his life abundant until he has built up a crumbling wall, paid off a heavy debt, enticed a disbeliever to his knees, filled an empty stomach, influenced a soul to wash in the blood of the Lamb, turned fear and frustration into peace and sureness, led one to be "born again."

One is measuring up to his opportunity potential when he has saved a crumbling marriage, transformed the weak into the strong, changed a civil to a temple marriage, brought enemies from the cesspool of hate to the garden of love, made a child trust and love him, changed a scoffer into a worshiper, melted a stony heart into one of flesh and muscle. (*The Teachings of Spencer W. Kimball,* pp. 249–50.)

In a commencement address to a class of high school graduates in Arizona, President Kimball made the following remarks that seem to me to be an excellent description of his own full life of service:

On the other hand, I know another man who has never given thought to himself. His every desire was for the protection and pleasure of those about him. No task was too great, no sacrifice too much for him to make for his fellowmen. His means brought relief from physical suffering; his kind work and thoughtfulness brought comfort and cheer and courage. Wherever people were in distress, he was on hand, cheering the discouraged, burying the dead, comforting the bereaved, and proving himself a friend in need. His time, his means, and his energies were lavished upon those needing assistance. Having given of himself freely, by that same act he has added to his mental, physical, and moral stature until today he stands in his declining years a power for good, an example and an inspiration to many. He has developed and grown until he is everywhere acclaimed, loved, and appreciated. He has given life and in a real way has truly found the abundant life. (*The Teachings of Spencer W. Kimball,* p. 251.)

In the Old Testament, we are asked, "And who then is willing to consecrate his service this day unto the Lord?" (1 Chronicles 29:5.)

Paul in the New Testament asks that "ye present your bodies a living sacrifice, holy, acceptable unto God, which is your reasonable service" (Romans 12:1).

That counsel is consistent with the many times we are invited by the Lord to serve with everything we have: "Therefore, O ye that embark in the service of God, see that ye serve him with all your heart, might, mind and strength, that ye may stand blameless before God at the last day" (D&C 4:2).

A returned missionary said: "After I got home from my mission and was spending most of my time thinking about myself, I lost something until I recognized that King Benjamin's message in the Book of Mormon was as true for me today as back when he said that if we are to serve God, we needed to serve our fellow men (see Mosiah 2:17). I finally realized that I wasn't released from that responsibility when I arrived home. I decided that I should do at least one thing every day to be of service to someone else who needed me. Things seemed to open up in my schedule and I found ways to find time to help others. From then on, the Spirit came back into my life in a special way."

The returned missionary who comes to recognize that we need to help "the poor and needy" all the time makes an important discovery. Those who are poor could use help in almost every way. Also, it is important to realize that even though all the poor are needy, not all the needy are poor. There are those who may be living in well-fixed economic circumstances who need a friend, a visit, encouragement, or help to become more active.

You should be innovative and find ways to serve without having to be assigned by someone else. The Lord has said, "Verily I say, men should be anxiously engaged in a good cause, and do many things of their own free will, and bring to pass much righteousness" (D&C 58:27).

Service can be given in almost any way. Some need help physically. A college student had been in an accident and was confined to a wheelchair. An acquaintance, without any formal assignment, made sure that he was regularly waiting at the door of the classroom when the wheelchair traveler needed to get across campus to his next class. They had a good visit along the way.

One crisp morning when the temperature was near zero, a few minutes before a seven o'clock class, I saw two coeds walking slowly on each side of a young friend who was making her way with crutches—one in each hand. They were going toward class. I was impressed with the attitude of those serving in this selfless way, because on the campus in Rexburg, Idaho, there is a lot of snow in the winter. The sidewalks become slippery, and sometimes it isn't easy to walk even when you don't have any physical problems. On days when it snows, it is impressive to see able-bodied students take time from their schedules and make themselves available to help those whose feet and legs don't work normally.

I know of another busy student who, on her own and without any specific assignment, has taken an hour each day to read to a ninety-three year old widower whose eyesight is failing him. She read fourteen books to this brother during one academic year. She feels she also has been richly blessed as a result of her significant service.

President Kimball wisely observed: "Only when you lift a burden, God will lift your burden. Divine paradox this! The man who staggers and falls because his burden is too great can lighten that burden by taking on the weight of another's burden. You get by giving, but your part of giving must be given first." (*The Teachings of Spencer W. Kimball*, p. 251.)

At Ricks College the students have created programs that provide many opportunities for service. One of them is called the "Big Buddy" program, in which college students are assigned to children of their same gender—that is, young men to boys and young women to girls—in homes where there is a single parent. Each week they arrange their schedules to spend a few hours in activities such as— in the case of the male gender—teaching young boys who don't have fathers in their homes how to catch and throw a ball, fish, ride a horse, study better, tie knots for Scouting, or whatever seems most appropriate and most needed under the circumstances. The young women big buddies similarly gear their teaching to girls' interests. One returned missionary said, "I never resented giving of my time. It is good to know that I am doing something that really is appreciated by the boy and also the mother. I feel better than when I do something that merely benefits me. This service helps me to appreciate a lot of things I have always taken for granted back at home with my own family."

Another returned missionary found time to help students with physical handicaps have some recreational experiences they probably would not have had in any other way through the student organization for handicapped students. With specially designed equipment, young adults with a wide variety of physical problems experience the thrill of such activities as skiing, camping, water-skiing, horseback riding, and river rafting. Self-confidence and self-esteem are enhanced among those who generally are left out of such activities. The lives of the handicapped are enriched, but more often than not, those without physical handicaps who give of themselves are helped to grow as much or more.

Another area of great service potential is with those who are less active. In every ward of the Church there are those who need more encouragement and involvement. Check with your elders quorum president or the bishop of the ward to see if there are some whom you could help to bring back into greater activity.

It is not just in the mission field that the following scripture applies: "If it so be that you should labor all your days in crying repentance unto this people, and bring, save it be one soul unto me, how great shall be your joy with him in the kingdom of my Father! And now, if your joy will be great with one soul that you have brought unto me into the kingdom of my Father, how great will be your joy if you should bring many souls unto me!" (D&C 18:15–16.)

Actively serving will strengthen you spiritually and in many other ways. President Kimball observed that "the most vital thing we can do is to express our testimonies through service, which will, in turn, produce spiritual growth, greater commitment, and a greater capacity to keep the comandments" (*The Teachings of Spencer W. Kimball*, p. 254).

Service is at the heart of the gospel of Jesus Christ. The Lord has promised that you who will lose yourselves in the service of others will actually find yourselves. You will discover that turning out to others and their needs will benefit not only them, but you also will find great personal satisfaction in rendering the service. As you make the adjustment from full-time missionary service to the Lord to a continuing concern for service to others at every opportunity that presents itself, you will be helped to make an effective adjustment to being back from your mission. In that way you will receive the satisfaction that comes from knowing that you are really in the service of your God.

Service to others is one of your most effective avenues to a rapid and positive adjustment from your mission to habits that will carry you through the rest of your life.

Conclusion

Well, now you are home and your future lies before you. Fortunately, that future is a lot brighter because of your service as a missionary. Whatever you may have accomplished before you filled your calling will be outdistanced by what you can do now with the added experience, refinement, and maturity that accompany full-time service in the name of—and authorized by—the Lord Jesus Christ.

While you served your mission, you presented vital gifts to those you taught. Those who were converted and baptized received a blessing worth more than mortal life itself. President Stephen L Richards spoke of these gifts when he said:

> What has been given? Why, to every man what he needed. To the poor, they who are so many, the gospel of thrift; to the rich, who are so few, the

gospel of giving; to the intemperate, the gospel of self control; to the indolent the gospel of work; to the downcast the gospel of hope; to the militant the gospel of peace; to the ignorant freedom from superstition; to the cynical and the wavering a vital, satisfying philosophy; to the sinner the gospel of repentance; and to all faith, purity, idealism, happiness and exaltation. (In Conference Report, April 1930, p. 106.)

Having the privilege of presenting such vital gifts to others will warm your memory for as long as you will be able to remember anything in this life and even into the life beyond the veil.

You have presented gifts of inestimable value, and you have also received them. Several years ago, I sat in an audience of newly called mission presidents and their wives listening intently to marvelous counsel delivered by members of the First Presidency and other General Authorities. President Gordon B. Hinckley spoke to us from his heart and his vast experience as a missionary and leader in the Church. Among other ideas, he shared with us a list of ten such gifts he hoped that missionaries would bring home with them from their missions. They were:

1. A love for and knowledge of God the Father and Jesus Christ.
2. A love for the scriptures.
3. A love and appreciation for parents.
4. A love for the people in the mission in which they served.
5. An understanding of the availability and reality of inspiration.
6. Humility in prayer.
7. A knowledge of how to work, work, work.

8. A knowledge of the importance of teamwork.
9. An increased faith.
10. A strengthened testimony.
("Ten Gifts Each Missionary Will Bring Back.")

I hope you have brought these gifts home with you. If so, your adjustment and chances for success and happiness in the future are very promising indeed.

Welcome home!

Sources Cited

Bennett, William J. "The Humanities: We Must Reclaim Our Heritage." *Private Colleges.* 1986.

Black, Susan Easton. *Finding Christ Through the Book of Mormon.* Salt Lake City: Deseret Book Co., 1987.

Bloom, Allan. *The Closing of the American Mind.* New York: Simon and Schuster, 1987.

Caldwell, Taylor. *A Pillar of Iron.* Greenwich, Connecticut: Fawcett Publications, 1982.

Christensen, Joe J. *To Grow in Spirit.* Salt Lake City: Deseret Book Co., 1983.

Conference Reports of The Church of Jesus Christ of Latter-day Saints. Salt Lake City: The Church of Jesus Christ of Latter-day Saints, October 1922, April 1930, April 1934, October 1973, October 1981, April 1988.

Davenport, Effie. "It's the Language of Angels." *The Rexburg Standard Journal: The Weekender.* 18 August 1988.

de Azevedo, Lex. *Pop Music and Morality.* North Hollywood, California: Embryo Books, 1982.

Deseret News, 17 June 1944.

Durant, Will and Ariel. *The Lessons of History.* New York: Simon and Schuster, 1968.

Ensign, December 1971, January 1974, April 1974, May 1980, January 1981, April 1982.

Gibbons, Francis. *Heber J. Grant: Man of Steel, Prophet of God.* Salt Lake City: Deseret Book Co., 1979.

Hinckley, Gordon B. "Ten Gifts Each Missionary Will Bring Back with Him." Notes of an address given 24 June 1983, Mission Presidents' Seminar.

Journal of Discourses. 26 vols. London: Latter-day Saints' Book Depot, 1854–86.

Kimball, Spencer W. "Chastity." Address delivered 2 January 1959.

———. *The Miracle of Forgiveness.* Salt Lake City: Bookcraft, 1969.

———. *The Teachings of Spencer W. Kimball.* Edited by Edward L. Kimball. Salt Lake City: Bookcraft, 1982.

King, Arthur Henry. *The Abundance of the Heart.* Salt Lake City: Bookcraft, 1986.

Lock, Robert D. *Taking Charge of Your Career Direction: Career Planning Guidebook, Book 1.* Pacific Grove, California: Brooks/Cole Publishing Co., 1988.

Lurie, Joseph, comp. "America . . . Globally Blind, Deaf and Dumb." *Foreign Language Annals* 15 (1982): 413–21.

Madsen, John M. "Church Activity of Returned Missionaries." Ph.D. dissertation, Brigham Young University, 1977.

Millennial Star, 27 July 1933.

Molloy, John T. "Clothes Power." *Boardroom Reports.* 15 December 1976.

———. *Dress for Success.* New York: Peter H. Wyden, 1976.

New Era, July 1971, September 1974, January 1978.

Packer, Boyd K. *"That All May Be Edified."* Salt Lake City: Bookcraft, 1982.

Peale, Norman Vincent. *Sin, Sex and Self-Control.* Greenwich, Connecticut: Fawcett Publications, 1965.

Priesthood Bulletin, December 1970.

Scroll, 28 September 1988.

Smith, Joseph. *History of The Church of Jesus Christ of Latter-day Saints.* Edited by B. H. Roberts. 7 vols. Salt Lake City: The Church of Jesus Christ of Latter-day Saints, 1932–51.

"Standards for Dating." Nonpublished manuscript produced by the Yuba City California Stake.

Tate, Lucile C. *LeGrand Richards: Beloved Apostle.* Salt Lake City: Bookcraft, 1982.

Thourlby, William. *You Are What You Wear: The Key to Business Success.* Kansas City: Sheed Andrews and McMeel, Inc., 1978.

Tingey, Lowell. "Celestial Dating." Nonpublished manuscript produced by the Yuba City California Stake.

Widtsoe, John A. *Evidences and Reconciliations.* Arranged by G. Homer Durham. Salt Lake City: Bookcraft, 1987.

Wolfe, Thomas. *You Can't Go Home Again.* New York: Harper and Brothers, 1934.

Young, Brigham. *Discourses of Brigham Young.* Selected by John A. Widtsoe. Salt Lake City: Deseret Book Co., 1954.

Index

Index

Technical schools, 49

Television, on Sabbath day, 73; worldwide missionary tool, 106

Television programs, inappropriate, 33

Temple, setting for inspiration, 51–52

Temple attendance, 73, 103

Temple marriage, statistics on, 67–68

Temple recommend, statistics regarding, 67–68; use of, 73

Temporal duties, inspiration regarding, 65

Temptation, 74; overcoming, 68–69; through immodesty, 35–36

Testimony, bearing in second language, 18; element of welcome-home address, 14, 16; helping family members gain, 11; opportunities for sharing, 63; responsibility to share, 76, 79; strengthened through mission service, 125; strengthened through service, 122; strengthened through study, 61; taught by mothers, 28; to be shared in language of congregation, 18–19; weakening of, 69–70

Thoughts, virtuous, 38

Thourlby, William, on dress and grooming, 41

Time, wise use of, 74–76

Time limit, marrying within, 23–24

Tingey, Lowell, on influence of movies, 33

Tithing, failure to pay, 70; statistics on, 68

Traditions, family, 10

Training, received on mission, 4

Travelogue, inappropriate in sacrament meeting, 14

Trustworthiness, indicated by dress and grooming, 41

Truth, learned through study of humanities, 59; testimony of, 18

Twain, Mark, on value of reading, 58

— U —

Unfaithfulness, in marriage, 22

Unhappiness, sin a source of, 74; through loss of spirituality, 70

Unity, striving for, 78

University, selection of, 52

"University of the Lord," mission referred to as, 4

— V —

Vessels of light, missionaries to become, 4

Videos, inappropriate, 33

Violence, in movies, 33

Virtue, maintained through dating standards, 38

Vocational education, 56–57

— W —

Weight control, importance of, 93–94

Welcome-home address, suggestions for, 13–18

Western civilizations, study of, 59

Wholeheartedness, in service to God, 119

Widower, assisted by student, 120

Widtsoe, John A., on spiritual knowledge, 61

Wife, importance of homemaking skills, 27

Will power, in weight control, 93–94

Wisdom, in dating, 32–38

Wolfe, Thomas, 8–9

Word of Christ, feasting on, 77

Word of Wisdom, health teachings in, 92; statistics on, 68

Work, importance of, 48, 77, 78, 124

Worship, through music, 87–88

— Y —

Young, Brigham, on guidance of Holy Ghost, 65; on value of spiritual learning, 60–61

Young women, mission an opportunity for, 97–98

Youth, setting example for, 16